SKITS
for children

SKITS
for children

Sheila Kitchens
with illustrations by Lisa Yost

Rutledge Books, Inc.  Bethel, CT

Copyright© 1996 by Sheila Kitchens

ALL RIGHTS RESERVED
Rutledge Books, Inc.
8 F.J. Clarke Circle, Bethel, CT 06801

Manufactured in the United States of America

Cataloging in Publication Data
    Kitchens, Sheila.
        Skits For Children/Sheila Kitchens ; with illustrations by Lisa Yost.
        p. cm.
        ISBN 1-887750-21-5
        1. Children's plays, American. 2. Knock-knock jokes.
I. Yost, Lisa. II. Title.
812.54--dc20   96-69513

ACKNOWLEDGMENTS

To God be the Glory great things he has done. Without his guiding hands this accomplishment could not have been achieved. There were many times I felt as though I would never find the time to complete this work.

One day I found myself deep in thought about my work when my son called and asked me to bring his football gear to school that he had left at home. On the drive to school my thoughts wandered to the book. I prayed asking if this was the right thing for me to do. My other commitments seemed to be more important and kept taking me away from what I wanted to do. I vented my frustrations and concerns about not being able to find the time to go through my material and choose the right ones to include in my writings. I left it in the Lord's hands. I didn't know which way to go.

After I parked the van and got out, I asked the Lord to give me a sign to continue my work: Let me know if this is what You want me to do. On my walk up to the school I happened to look down on the ground and I found my answer. There, no bigger than a half-inch, was a yellow smiley face staring up at me. He had given me His answer.

From that point on I worked on this compilation every chance I got. To my scouting friends I say thank you. You were such a great influence on my efforts. To my family I say I love you for caring enough to support me in my quest.

I dedicate this book to those people who's job it is to entertain others through humorous drama. I hope and pray that you will find just the right skit to captivate your audience and that the young people have fun putting it on.

God Bless all of you.

In Christian Love, Sheila.

CONTENTS

INTRODUCTION
Opening, Props, Scenery iii
Make-Up, Costumes, Areas Of Concern iv
Let's Write A Skit vi

IT'S SHOW TIME!
Baseball Throwing Contest 2
Kayak Trouble 2
Railroad Crossing 3
The Atlantic Trip 4
The Infantry 5
There Is A Bear 6
Torn Paper 7
Bon Voyage 8
Lion Tamer 8
Defective Nails 9
Bird Watching Pun 10
Weary Traveler 11
Buc Tuocs 12
The Six Ships Of Scouting 13
The Other Side Of The Mountain 14
Bird Watchers 15
The Redcoats Are Coming! 16
Helping Hands 16
The Flea Circus 17
The Special Picnic 18
Freedom 19
Balloon Madness 20
Hillbilly Family 21
Peace Be With You 21
All Aboard! 22
Baked Alaska 23
The Liberty Bell 24
On The Line 26
Extra, Extra! 26

General Custer 27
Beach Bummer 27
Pumpkin Pie Patch 28
Broken Lawnmower 30
Higher Court 31
Christmas Carols 32
Vindow Viper 33
Wrong Feet 33
Jelly Beans 34
A Fool's Gold 36
Confused Drummer 38
Many Muscles 39
I Am An American 40
Some Beach 41
Welcome To Our Neighborhood 42
This Is Your Life! 43
The Forgotten Treasure 45
Christmas Around The World 46
God Bless America 47
Nature's Beauty 49
How The Turkey Got His Name 50
What Time Is It? 51
How Do You Get To Spunkerville? 52
Stiff Neck 53
Bawl Game 53
The Christmas Present 54
Order In The Court Room 56
Shake Well 57
Those Important Papers 58

RUN-ONS AND KNOCK-KNOCK JOKES
A collection of over 40 run-ons and jokes 60

INDEX 69

INTRODUCTION

The following is a collection of skits that are designed to help you when you need a quickie stunt or ice breaker. Skits come in many forms. They have different names depending on the job they are doing. In addition to skit, they are known as audience participation, run-ons, stunts, pantomimes, plays, charades, and slap stick.

The actors are the key to the skit. They are the boys and girls who jump at the chance to ham it up and perform in front of their friends and parents. Children love to use their imaginations, so when the opportunity arises, let them take part in writing parts of the skit. They will enjoy participating if they feel the skit is part theirs.

It is through their acting that the story is reveled. They practice their lines and their actions, then the skit is presented on a "live" stage. Performing on a stage in front of an audience takes a lot of courage. It is not easy for an eight or nine year old child to stand up in front of an audience and talk. With the use of costumes, make-up, props and scenery, it makes it possible for even the shy child to participate and have fun.

Doing skits help to teach many important qualities:
- A child learns to "listen." To follow instructions given by the director is a must for all actors. Listen to know what is expected from you and the others. Each person has a different role in making the skit a success, so listening is important for everyone.
- A child will learn to "vocalize" himself. He will be able to express his part of the skit by how he speaks. Through practice he will be taught the need to speak loud enough for the audience to hear him and slow enough to be understood.
- A child will learn "teamwork." It takes everybody working together to perform the skit. All parts are equally important and no one part or person should be more emphasized.
- A child will learn "respect." The child will learn to respect the director for who he is and what he is trying to do. He will also respect the fellow actors for their part in the skit and their interest in doing their best. And they will also learn to respect the amount of time needed to create the scenery and props, and the work put into them to get them ready for the skit.

- Then a child will learn "pride." After making all the scenery and props, practicing lines and movement, getting fitted for costumes, and then going out on stage for this short five minute skit, a child will feel a sense of pride in knowing that it was a success because he gave his best.

Props

Props are used to help set the scene. They are a vital part of the program because they help the audience to better visualize the skit. What you use as a prop will largely be determined on the size of your stage area. This could be an open floor, a platform at one end of the room, or a real stage set-up as found in schools. Consider what kind of lighting you will have and if you will have access to use it. Check for built-in microphones and locate the electrical outlets if you plan to use a tape recorder or any special effects.

A prop can be a chair, cardboard box, or a cane. A sign to identify the character can be as effective as a costume. Props can also be a box, mustache, eye patch, bandanna, and a cardboard sword for a pirate. Football helmet, baseball glove, balloons, or binoculars can be used for a day at the games. Paper bag vests, cowboy hats, Indian feathers, Indian beads, and wood for a pretend fire are needed for Cowboys and Indians. Grocery bags, a mailbox, a small table, a lamp, a wig, mother's dress, father's suit coat, or shoes are useful for a home type setting.

An outstanding feature we do not want to sidestep is the use of sound effects. It will boost the mood and grab the attention of the audience when used. Good sound effects are bicycle horn, the sound of drums beating, the roar of animals coming from offstage, the ticking of a clock, a cookie sheet or piece of aluminum for a crack of thunder. Homemade musical instruments made by the children and played by them will add jazz to the scene. A pre-recording played from a recorder works well.

Scenery

Scenery helps to make the skit more believable. It's fun to make and a good project for all the children to take part. Refrigerator boxes and washing machine boxes cut open make great back drops. Use old sheets strung between poles made of PVC pipe or large pieces of corrugated cardboard. Boxes of all sizes can be used and cut to any shape. Add tempera paints, crayons, markers, yarn, colored paper, raffia, glitter, pictures, material, and

Introduction

other items to help with the final design. Use gray colors for a sad effect and bright colors for a happy effect.

Make-Up

Make-up helps to change the child's own features. It can make the face appear older, lips larger, eyes brighter, or can make a face look happy or sad. Make-up can alter the character totally and will generally bring out the best in the child playing the part.

Use cornstarch powdered in the hair to make a person look older. Eyebrow pencil can darken or change the shape of the eyebrow. You can also use it on the bridge of the nose to change it's shape. Use nose putty to make a big nose or cover up your own eyebrows. It can also be used to change the shape of the ears and make warts. Eye shadow used under the eye gives a sunken hollow effect. Black crayon can be used to stimulate a missing tooth. Lipstick can be used to make lips darker or give a sunburn effect to the face. New looking wounds can be drawn with lipstick or fingernail polish. Old scars can be drawn with eyebrow pencil and powdered over. For a bald man, use an old bathing cap (white or flesh) for the base then glue on yarn for hair around the edge. For a curly haired person, start with that old bathing cap. Cut colored paper into 1/2 inch strips and curl using a pencil. Curl several times for a tight curl then glue or tape them to the bathing cap. To make braids use crepe paper. Gently stretch the strips of paper and twist them. Secure the ends with a paper clip. Take 3 of the twisted strips and braid them together, stapling the ends. For Indian braids, use black paper. Glasses made from wire look most realistic. For a hillbilly or scarecrow, glue or tape uneven lengths of heavy cotton rug yarn to the inside of an old hat.

Here are two recipes for a base make-up.
- A clown base can be made using items found at home. Use equal parts of liquid cleansing cream and sifted powdered sugar. Mix until blended. To add color use a few drops of food coloring. This make-up wipes off easily. Keep extra tissues or paper towels for cleaning up messes.
- Another good base is to mix one tablespoon of shortening and two tablespoons of cornstarch with a fork until mixture is soft and creamy. Use a few drops of food coloring to tint. This mixture will keep in a baby food jar for days before drying out.

Use red for Indians; green for a monster; yellow, green, or blue for a spaceman; white for the base of a clown face. Apply make-up to the child AFTER they are dressed in their costume. Take make-up off BEFORE they take the costume off.

Costumes

A costume can be as simple or elaborate as the actor or actress would like them. Cloth costumes can be very durable, but they cost more. On the other hand, simple costuming can be made with things you can find around the house.

Costumes can be made from old clothing handed down from mom, dad, brother or sister. Don't throw away those old tights, tee-shirts, old robes, or felt hats. Save feathers and use as trim for knights costumes and Indians; old pop guns that do not work for the cowboys; foil for deputy badges and space costumes; vinyl for vests for the old west costumes. Old colored sheets can become dresses or wraps for a king or queen.

A clown, robot, animals, and a fat man can all be created out of an old box. Cut holes for the arms and legs and the head. Paint with tempera paints and trim with markers. Paper sacks can be used for costumes or masks. Save large brown sacks for all kinds of uses. Paint with tempera paints in the same fashion as the boxes. In fact, paints add strength to the paper sack when it is used in moderate proportions.

Areas Of Concern

Keep these rules in mind to help avoid problems.
- Keep the props and costumes simple.
- Keep the skit short, about three to five minutes is a good length.
- Avoid long, memorized lines, the children just can not do it.
- Let everyone participate in some way, don't forget anyone.
- Use stage directions. Make sure everyone knows where to go and what to do.
- Be sure the audience can hear the skit, and when it is appropriate, have the children look at the audience as they speak.
- Be careful not to let the more capable child do all the work.
- Children like to pretend, but they don't like to be sissies—change up any character to fit the needs of the child.

Introduction

Let's Write A Skit

There may be a time that you are asked to do a skit that you have not seen any material on. It will then be up to you and the children to sit down and put together your own skit. A skit can be based on a personal experience, a joke, or cartoon. Think of situations that are funny or embarrassing and dramatize it. You can focus on proud moments, exciting thrills, sovereign activities, or mistakes made by you or others.

There are five steps to consider when writing your own skit; Theme, Setting, Characters, Props, and Dialog. The following are some guidelines that will help you put together your own skit, or even change one to fit your needs.

- **Consider the theme:** Before planning any event, you need to know what the theme is. A theme may already be planned or you may be able to choose one you like. Some themes that are fun to work with are Mardi Gras, Hawaiian Luau, Along The Sea Shore, Adventures In The Backyard, Space, Dinosaurs, Dragons, Living In The Future, Looking At The Past, Sights And Sounds, Talent Show, and many others. I'm sure you have a favorite subject you could draw on for a theme. This now is your foundation, from here you will build your skit.

- **Choose the setting:** Based on the theme, the setting could be the city, the mountains, a street corner, a desert, the country, a haunted house, a bakery, a child's room, Christmas time, a party, the jungle, famous heroes, a boat trip, an old castle, the beach, a court room, or a railroad station. Don't forget about any special lighting effects or any music you may want to use. Consider all possibilities for your setting.

- **Choose the characters:** Who or what is the main character? How many people are needed to help execute the skit? What kind of make-up is needed to change the children into these characters? Consider the child's own character and what they can handle before asking them to play a part in the skit. The number of people available to work in the skit will determine the size of your cast. Try to include all people you are working with in one way or another in the skit as characters, prop builders, ushers at the door, or even the announcer.

- **Choose the props:** Props need to be simple and easy enough for the children to pick up and move around. Based on the theme and characters, choose props that will help emphasize the setting. Not many are needed—just enough to set the scene.

• **Add dialogue to your idea**: Considering the above ideas you now need to create the dialogue for your characters. First start with an outline of what you want to do and where you want to end up. Create a situation and then consider how it will be solved. Example:

>Here is your theme: Sea Of Adventures
>This is your situation: There is a hidden treasure off the far coast.
>Who is involved: A Captain, a First Mate, a Lookout, several Maties.
>How will it be solved: Children sail to the far coast; follow the treasure map; dig around area; find the treasure chest.
>How will it end: Open the chest to reveal the American flag—a perfect opening to any meeting.

With this outline, adding the dialogue will be easy. Use your imagination and have fun! And remember, let the children take part in writing the skits.

IT'S SHOWTIME!

BASEBALL THROWING CONTEST

SETTING: One person is selected to be the leader. He is holding a baseball in his hand with palm side up. Use as many other people as you want, but make sure each of them have a baseball that they can hold. Appoint one to do a speaking part with the person holding the ball.
SCENE: The person holding the ball is in the center of the room. When ready to start, have the other people walk in with their balls and go to the person in the center.

PERSON HOLDING BALL: I bet I can throw this ball as hard or as soft as I want and it will come back to me. Can you do the same and have your ball come back to you?

OTHER PERSONS: (They look inquistively to each other and each person, one at a time should roll or gently toss their ball to the side. Of course, it will not come back.)

SPEAKING PERSON: Our balls did not come back. What makes you so sure your ball will come back?

PERSON HOLDING BALL: Because I'll throw my ball in the air! (He gently tosses it up and it comes back to his hand.)

KAYAK TROUBLE

SETTING: Seven people are needed for speaking parts. For every two people you need one cardboard shaped kayak–type boat that they can hold in front of them. Appoint one to be the announcer. You need two twigs for each kayak.
SCENE: All kayaks on stage with two people in each one. The people need to be facing each other. The announcer does not come on until the very end.

It's Showtime!

FIRST PERSON: (Looks around.) Boy, this is nice up here!

SECOND PERSON: (Looking around, then points.) Sure is. Look there, a big elephant seal!

THIRD PERSON: Yes, and we just passed a whole bunch of seals swimming.

FOURTH PERSON: (Starts rubbing arms like shivering.) I am cold.

FIFTH PERSON: Yea, I'm kinda cold, too.

SIXTH PERSON: O.K. everyone, it's time to do it.

(Each kayak brings out twigs and holds them up just a little [try not to show your hands] and pretends to light them. People act like they are getting warm. In a few seconds, the kayaks start tipping over, one by one. Just have the people lay on their side with the cardboard kayak on top of them. Announcer, walks in and says in a loud voice....)

ANNOUNCER: The moral of our story is.....You can't have your kayak and heat it too!

RAILROAD CROSSING

SETTING: One person is selected as the First Leader and one is selected as the End Leader with as many other people as you want.
SCENE: Have all people stand side by side as close as possible. Place a cardboard set of railroad tracks in front of the people. Make it as long as the line of people. The person who is the End Leader needs to carry a clipboard or note pad.

FIRST LEADER: (Looks up and down the tracks, then turns to the person next to him.) Hey, is there a train coming from the North?

(Each person in turn will ask the person next to him the question asked by the First Leader. When it gets down to the End Leader, he will look at his clipboard, flip a page or two then respond.)

END LEADER: Nope, no train from the North.

(Each person in turn will relay the message back to the First Leader.)

FIRST LEADER: (Looks up and down the tracks, then turns to the one next to him.) Hey, is there a train coming from the South?

(Each person in turn will ask the person next to him the question asked by the First Leader. When it gets down to the End Leader, he will look at his clipboard, flip a page or two then respond.)

END LEADER: Nope, no train from the South.

(Each person in turn will relay the message back to the First Leader.)

(This continues for the East and West. Then the First Leader will say...)

FIRST LEADER: O.K. then, let's all cross the tracks now. (Everyone steps over the tracks.)

THE ATLANTIC TRIP

SETTING: Four to six people with one selected as the Captain. Have the Captain wear a Captain's hat. Make a ship's rail out of a large washing machine box painted brown.
SCENE: The Captain and the people are leaning on the rail as the Captain is telling them about the journey. As the trip is explained, the people begin to feel sick.

CAPTAIN: This is one of the nicer trips on the oceans. Our course will take us up and down the Atlantic coast. As far south as South America where the waters are pretty calm and nice and warm. Up north to the coastal waters off Virginia where the waters start getting a little rough and we must be careful to keep the ship steady. As we come close to shore the waves have a tendency to rock our ship a little.

(The people begin to look worried and a little sick.)

CAPTAIN: As we get closer to the north the waters become very cold and icy. They are not as rough as the mid Atlantic, but we can feel a little disturbance from time to time as the waters shift and move around us as the ocean floor changes. The icebergs can cause some problems. When we veer to miss them

It's Showtime!

and still get too close, they can tip the ship as much as 30 degrees. (People start leaning over the rail, feeling sick. Except the second person who this does not seem to effect.)

FIRST PERSON: Look, Captain. What is that? (pointing)

CAPTAIN: That is the tip of a volcano that has erupted and the ash and lava have run down the sides.

SECOND PERSON: Oh, yeah! Like when you eat too much and you erupt?

(All but the Captain and the second person start to look sicker and run off stage holding their mouths.)

THE INFANTRY

SETTING: Five people are needed with one being selected to carry a small tree and shovel.

SCENE: Each person will enter the stage area from different directions or different areas of the room if possible. The one with the tree should be offstage and come on last.

FIRST PERSON: (He comes running in and yelling.) The infantry is coming! The infantry is coming! (Stops in center of stage.)

SECOND PERSON: (He comes running in and yelling.) The infantry is coming! The infantry is coming! (Stops in center of stage.)

THIRD PERSON: (He comes running in and yelling.) The infantry is coming! The infantry is coming! (Stops in center of stage.)

FOURTH PERSON: (He comes running in and yelling.) The infantry is coming! The infantry is coming! (Stops in center of stage.)

(This continues with as many people as you have. When you get to the one carrying the tree, he comes walking in carrying the tree and shovel.)

LAST PERSON WITH TREE: The infant tree is here, where do we plant it?

THERE IS A BEAR

SETTING: It is a good idea for an adult to help lead this one but use as many people as you want.
SCENE: Have everyone line up as close together as possible but still able to use their arms.

FIRST PERSON: I see a bear!
SECOND PERSON: Where?
FIRST PERSON: Over there! (Points to the left with his right hand.)

SECOND PERSON: I see a bear!
THIRD PERSON: Where?
SECOND PERSON: Over there! (Points to the left with his right hand.)

THIRD PERSON: I see a bear!
FOURTH PERSON: Where?
THIRD PERSON: Over there! (Points to the left with his right hand.)

FOURTH PERSON: I see a bear!
FIFTH PERSON: Where?
FOURTH PERSON: Over there! (Points to the left with his right hand.)

(This continues until the last person is speaking.)

LAST PERSON: I see a bear!
FIRST PERSON: Where?
LAST PERSON: Over there! (Points to the left with his right hand.)

FIRST PERSON: I see a bear!
SECOND PERSON: Where?
FIRST PERSON: Over there! (Takes his left hand and crosses it over his right hand and points.)

It's Showtime!

(Continue in this manner until all people have done it and it has come back to the first person.)

FIRST PERSON: I see a bear!
SECOND PERSON: Where?
FIRST PERSON: Down there! (The first person will squat down. Hands stay crossed while squatting.)

(Continue in this manner until all people have done it and it has come back to the first person.)

FIRST PERSON: I see a bear!
SECOND PERSON: Where?
FIRST PERSON: Back there! (The first person will turn into the second person causing all of them to fall off balance and come tumbling down!)

TORN PAPER

SETTING: One person will act as the leader. Use as many other people as you want. Have a square piece of paper for each of them except the person acting as the leader.
SCENE: Have the leader at a table with the pieces of paper on it. The other people then enter.

LEADER: I bet you that you can not take a piece of paper and tear it into four equal parts.

FIRST PERSON: I think we can. It's easy to tear a piece of paper into four equal parts.

LEADER: Well, I don't think you can do it!

SECOND PERSON: If we show you it can be done, what will you give us?

LEADER: (Thinks for just a minute.) O.K., I'll give you each a quarter.

(The people look at each other and then reach for a piece of paper. They proceed to tear it into four equal parts. They fold the paper in half and creases the edge then opens and tears along the crease. Then they take the two pieces and folds each of them in half, creases, then tears.)

FIRST PERSON: See, we all have four equal pieces of paper. Now you owe each of us a quarter!

LEADER: O.K., so I do. (He picks up one piece of each of the people's torn paper and gives each of them a "quarter" of a piece of paper.) Here is your "Quarter." (He hands them a piece of paper.)

BON VOYAGE

SETTING: A large number of people work well with this skit. A cardboard cut-out of a large ocean cruise liner with an opening at both ends so the people can walk through.
SCENE: Have half of the people stand behind the ocean liner like they are leaving and have the others stand in front. All people are waving to each other and saying things like; "Have a nice trip," "Bon Voyage," "Hope you have a nice vacation," "See you later," "Call me when you get back," and so on.

On cue—have one person in the front say, "I need to shake your hand one more time!," and he runs ONTO the ship. At the same time have one person already on the ship say something similar and he runs OFF the ship. Give just a couple of seconds and do this again, with two other people. Each person is changing positions and going to shake the hand of the other person. This continues until all people have switched places....then start it again. Do this until the audience catches on and is laughing or until all people have had a chance to rotate.

LION TAMER

SETTING: One person with a five foot piece of rope to be used as a whip, a dummy chicken, and any other number of people with two selected to do speaking parts.
SCENE: The people are gathered around the one person with the rope who is making a whipping action at the chicken and mumbling words of command. In come the two speaking people.

FIRST PERSON: What is he doing?

SECOND PERSON: Practicing.

FIRST PERSON: Practicing what?

SECOND PERSON: He wants to be a lion tamer!

FIRST PERSON: (Walks over and looks at the chicken on the floor.) But that's not a lion, that's a chicken!

SECOND PERSON: So is he!

DEFECTIVE NAILS

SETTING: Two people with carpenter's aprons and two hammers.
SCENE: The two people come out and walk up to a wall and pretend to drive in nails. One carpenter takes out an imaginary nail, examines it, and throws it over his shoulder. He takes another nail out and drives it into the wall. Continue in this manner with the carpenter throwing some of the nails over his shoulder. After the third or fourth time the other person notices and comments...

FIRST PERSON: You're wasting nails! Look how many you have thrown away! Why are you throwing all those nails away?

SECOND PERSON: Those nails are defective. How am I supposed to build this wall with defective nails?

FIRST PERSON: Defective! What do you mean defective! (Reach over and pretend to pick up a few.) They look perfectly all right to me.

SECOND PERSON: Well, look here. The heads are on the wrong end of those nails! Anyone can see that! How am I suppose to drive these nails when they look like this?

FIRST PERSON: Dummy! Those nails are for the other side of the wall!

BIRD WATCHING PUN

SETTING: As many as ten people are needed with one of them being the announcer. Let the people pick the bird they want to be and then they are responsible for getting the props for that bird.
SCENE: All people in front with their props behind them. After they talk about their bird, continue to make the motions as all birds are introduced.

ANNOUNCER: Ladies and gentlemen, you all know that a "PUN" is a funny way of saying and showing something. With that in mind, let's have some "PUN" with birds.

FIRST PERSON: I am a "Pen"quin. (Holds up a fountain pen.) Ball point, that is.

SECOND PERSON: I am a Mockingbird. Ha, Ha, Ha. (Flap arms like wings of bird, turn around in place.) I am a Mockingbird. Ha, Ha, Ha. (Flap arms like wings of bird, turn around in place.)

THIRD PERSON: I am a "Rob"in. (Pulls out toy gun.) Hand over the worms!

FOURTH PERSON: I am a Coo-coo Bird. (Pulls out walnuts on a string.) I'm a nut, I'm a nut! (Starts to act silly. Narrator runs out with a white sheet or towel and wraps around his shoulders. He is still for the rest of the skit.)

FIFTH PERSON: I'm a Weather Bird. (Pulls out a picture of a TV.) You see me on the TV news every day.

SIXTH PERSON: I am a Yellow Warbler. (Wears a yellow tee-shirt and sing a line or two of a song.)

SEVENTH PERSON: I am a Cardinal. Play ball! (Pull out a bat and put over shoulder and have a ball in your hand.)

EIGHTH PERSON: I'm a Whip-Poor-Will. (Says the name real slow and has a whip in his hand.) O.K., where is Will?

NINTH PERSON: I'm a Cat Bird. I'm really confused. Tweet-tweet. Meow-meow. Tweet-tweet. Meow-meow.

ANNOUNCER: Well folks, that's all. I hope you'll forgive us. Oh, by the way....(pulls out a ball attached to a chain)....I'm a "Jail" Bird.

WEARY TRAVELER

SETTING: Five people are needed with one of them selected to be the "Weary Traveler." He needs to have with him a large piece of paper and a wide marker hidden in a pocket. Have others dress up to the part or just wear a sign around their neck to say who they are.

SCENE: The "Weary Traveler" enters the stage acting tired and lays down in the middle of the stage. He talks about walking so far, how tired he is, and thinks he'll just take a nap. Lays down to rest.

TELEPHONE REPAIRMAN: (Enters singing or humming a song.) I wonder what time it is. (Goes up to the traveler.) Excuse me, can you tell me what time it is?

WEARY TRAVELER: Sorry, I don't have a watch. I do not know what time it is. (Telephone repairman leaves.)

MAILMAN: Neither rain nor snow or dark of night will keep me from my appointed route. However, being late can hinder me. (Walks over to the traveler.) Mister, can you tell me what time it is?

WEARY TRAVELER: Sorry, I do not have a watch. I do not know what time it is. (Mailman leaves.)

TV REPORTER: I'mmmmmm Marvin Swindler and I have to do an interview at 4:00 and I don't have a watch to tell me the time. (Walks over to the traveler.) What time is it, sir?

WEARY TRAVELER: (Said with a little frustration.) I don't have a watch! I do not know what time it is. (Reporter leaves. The weary traveler pulls out paper and marker and makes a sign saying "I DO NOT HAVE A WATCH," lays it across his stomach and returns to his nap.)

PAPER BOY: (Enters whistling and slowly reads the sign.) Hey, mister (as he pokes at the traveler.) It is 5 o'clock. (Then he skips off.)

BUC TUOCS

SETTING: Seven boys are needed with one of them selected as the announcer. Need a stand alone mic so boys can talk into it.
SCENE: The boys are gathered around as the radio show is about to begin.

ANNOUNCER: (Into the mic.) Boys, have you been feeling a little sluggish lately? Do you have that gray feeling? Do you have that over-seven feeling? I have the answer to your woes! The name is "Buc Tuocs". We have with us tonight people who have tried Buc Tuocs and are wild about it. Here are our guests to tell you about it.

FIRST PERSON: When I reached eight, I needed something. I was out of touch. I tried "Buc Tuocs" and got the lift I needed.

SECOND PERSON: I couldn't adjust. My social life was falling apart. "Buc Tuocs" was the answer.

THIRD PERSON: I was plagued with the fear of growing old. Growing taller before my time. "Buc Tuocs" helped me to overcome my fear.

FOURTH PERSON: My life seemed to be passing me by. I could not find the right things to do. "Buc Tuocs" came to my rescue.

FIFTH PERSON: "Buc Tuocs" changed my life. New horizons were opened to me.

SIXTH PERSON: Girls were my problem. My kindergarten friends had gone in different directions. "Buc Tuocs" helped me to find new friends.

ANNOUNCER: Thank you, boys, for your excellent testimonials. Remember folks, try "Buc Tuocs" for all your needs. "Buc Tuocs," by the way, is "Cub Scout" spelled backwards.

It's Showtime!

THE SIX SHIPS OF SCOUTING

SETTING: Seven people are needed with one being selected as the announcer. Six poster boards with a sailing ship drawn on each one. In the center of each ship write the following words: SCHOLAR-SHIP, FELLOW-SHIP, FRIEND-SHIP, SPORTSMAN-SHIP, WORKMAN-SHIP, and STATES-MAN-SHIP.
   Read ahead of time about each one and be sure to put the proper flag on the ship. On the back of each poster write the words that the people have to say.
SCENE: Each person is on stage with his poster in front of him about waist high. As each person reads his, it should be raised to show that ship.

ANNOUNCER: Tonight, we would like to tell you about the Six Ships of Scouting. These are ships which were launched in America strong and mighty.....ships that will last forever.

FIRST PERSON: SCHOLAR-SHIP...This ship is very important on the Sea of Education. On her deck stand such officers as ambition, determination, intelligence, and application. Her flag bears the letter "A" and the "PLUS" sign.

SECOND PERSON: FELLOW-SHIP...This ship stands for good spirit, fine cooperation, and never failing unity. It's flag floats high...the flag of Scouting.

THIRD PERSON: FRIEND-SHIP...This is the most handsome ship of all. It is true blue and it's flag is golden...since friendship itself is golden.

FOURTH PERSON: SPORTSMANSHIP... This is the ship that's fair and square. It never veers from its course. It's flag is never at half mast.

FIFTH PERSON: WORKMAN-SHIP...This ship's every line, every part, every mast, represents the best that a person can give. It's flag bears a laurel wreath.

SIXTH PERSON: STATESMAN-SHIP...This ship represents wise guidance, constant counsel, unselfish interest and sincere endeavor. It's flag is white for purity.

ANNOUNCER: And there you have the six strong and sturdy ships to brave the sea. Six ships that together create a solid wall for Scouting.

THE OTHER SIDE OF THE MOUNTAIN

SETTING: Five to eight people with one selected as the leader. You need a rope long enough for all people or several shorter ropes tied together to make one big one. You also need a climbing pick for the leader. Other props might include goggles, boots, stocking caps, and coats.
SCENE: People are tied together and pretend to be climbing a mountain. Have the people lay on the floor in the middle of the stage and crawl as if they are climbing the mountain. As they go they can start to stand up some like the way they are standing up when they reach the top.

FIRST PERSON: (Leader.) It's not much farther now men. I can see the top of the mountain.

SECOND PERSON: I can't wait to see the whole world from the top.

THIRD PERSON: I'm hungry, I hope there's a restaurant up there.

FOURTH PERSON: I have never been to the top of such a high mountain.

THIRD PERSON: What kind of food is at the top of a mountain?

FIFTH PERSON: I have the flag to post so the whole world can see it, and us.

THIRD PERSON: Did we have to make reservations in advance?

FIRST PERSON: We've made it! I'm at the top. I see....

ALL CLIMBERS: (A little excited.) Yes, yes....

FIRST PERSON: I see, I see....

ALL CLIMBERS: (A bit more excited.) Yes, yes....

FIRST PERSON: (Disappointed.) The other side of the mountain.

BIRD WATCHERS

SETTING: You will need four people and space enough for the people to roam around.
SCENE: One person already looking around the room—up and down, under and over.

SECOND PERSON: Hi (person's name), what are you doing?

FIRST PERSON: Looking for my bird.

SECOND PERSON: A bird. I'll help you look for it. (He too, now starts looking around the room.)

THIRD PERSON: Hi there! What's going on?

SECOND PERSON: We are looking for (person's name) bird.

THIRD PERSON: I can help. (He begins to look around.)

FOURTH PERSON: What is everybody doing?

FIRST PERSON: We are trying to find my bird.

FOURTH PERSON: Well, I can help too. (He begins to look around, then stops.) Hold it just a minute! Now where did you lose your bird?

FIRST PERSON: It flew out my open window.

THIRD PERSON: Out the window!

SECOND PERSON: Then why are we looking in here?

FIRST PERSON: It's raining (or cold, or too hot, etc.) outside. The weather is better in here.

THE REDCOATS ARE COMING

SETTING: Five people are needed for speaking parts. Two of them need to have red coats to wear.
SCENE: Have each person come running in just a few seconds behind the one before.

FIRST PERSON: (Comes running in and yelling.) The Redcoats are coming! The Redcoats are coming: (Runs off stage.)

SECOND PERSON: (Comes running in and yelling.) The Redcoats are coming! The Redcoats are coming: (Runs off stage.)

THIRD PERSON: (Comes running in and yelling.) The Redcoats are coming! The Redcoats are coming: (Runs off stage.)

FOURTH & FIFTH PERSONS: (Comes walking in, looks around.) Hello, we are the Redcoats.

HELPING HANDS

SETTING: A chair, lots of clothes and toys scattered everywhere. A large box hidden off stage close by. Any number of people can take part.
SCENE: One person is sitting on the chair in the middle of the messy room. He is in deep thought. The other people come in to see him.

SECOND PERSON: Hi, there! What are you doing?

FIRST PERSON: Just thinking.

THIRD PERSON: Thinking about what?

FIRST PERSON: My invention.

FOURTH PERSON: Are you inventing something?

FIRST PERSON: Sure, I want to be famous like Alexander Graham Bell or Thomas Edison.

SECOND PERSON: What do you have in mind, maybe we can help. (All

It's Showtime!

people shake heads yes.)

FIRST PERSON: Really? Do all of you want to help?

ALL: Sure!

FIRST PERSON: O.K. (As he gets up.) First of all I need a big box. (Name of person), there should be one over there in that corner somewhere. Now I need (start naming off the toys in the floor) and some old rags. We can use my clothes for the rags. Put everything in the box.
(The people start picking up the toys and clothes and put them in the box.)

FIRST PERSON: (Looking around the room and then in the box.) Well, that just about takes care of that.

FOURTH PERSON: Takes care of what?

FIRST PERSON: My invention, I just invented a way to get my room cleaned before my mom gets home!

THE FLEA CIRCUS

SETTING: Six to eight people are needed. No special costumes. One is selected to be reading a newspaper.
SCENE: They are lying on their stomachs in the middle of the stage pretending to be watching something. The person with the newspaper is offstage.

FIRST PERSON: Wow! Did you see that!

SECOND PERSON: Look there, I can't believe he did that!

THIRD PERSON: This one over here is doing it on a motorcycle!

FOURTH PERSON: This one is carrying three on his back!

FIFTH PERSON: That one just jumped all the way over here!

SIXTH PERSON: Gee! I never saw anyone do that before!

(The person with the newspaper enters and pretends to be reading as he is walking. He walks over to where the other people are and steps in the place that they are watching and continues to walk off stage. The group says nothing or does nothing)

THIRD PERSON: (Sitting up.) Boy, that was a good flea circus! (Other people sit up.)

FIRST PERSON: Yeah, and what a smashing finish!

THE SPECIAL PICNIC

SETTING: Six people are needed, all with paper sacks. In the center of the stage there should be a blanket to lay out on.
SCENE: In the backyard, all people just laying and standing around.

FIRST PERSON: Gee, there's nothing to do.

SECOND PERSON: Yeah, I know.

THIRD PERSON: Hey, let's have a backyard picnic!

FOURTH PERSON: But it may rain. It always rains when you start to have fun!

THIRD PERSON: I don't think so. If it does, we can eat in the house.

FIFTH PERSON: I'll bring some potato chips.

FIRST PERSON: I'll bring the hot dogs.

SECOND PERSON: I'll bring some drinks.

FOURTH PERSON: I'll bring the hot dog buns.

SIXTH PERSON: I'll bring something special!

(All walk offstage and come back carrying sacks.)

It's Showtime!

FIFTH PERSON: Here are the potato chips.

FIRST PERSON: Here's the hot dogs.

SECOND PERSON: I have the drinks.

FOURTH PERSON: I have the hot dog buns.

SIXTH PERSON: OH, NO! (Drops his sack.)

THIRD PERSON: What's wrong?

SIXTH PERSON: I brought something special all right, I brought the ants!

FREEDOM

SETTING: Eight people with one being selected to be the announcer. You will need half sheets of poster board with the word "Freedom" on one and a picture to represent each of the other symbols in the skit. Have the words they need to read written on the back of the poster.
SCENE: People come on stage in order and one at a time hold up their posters and read what is on the back. They should not lower their posters when done, keep them raised. The dialogue is in rhyme.

ANNOUNCER: (Freedom) We are here to tell you about the symbols of Freedom in the United States. We have come to cherish their meanings in our hearts. These symbols are the constant reminders of these privileges.

FIRST PERSON: (Statue of Liberty) For people of all other lands; the Statue of Liberty stands; with her flaming torch high; against America's sky; promising freedom from tyrant's demands.

SECOND PERSON: (Flag) Over the land of the free, flying high; Old Glory waves in the sky; thirteen stripes, fifty stars this banner is ours; to defend it, our heroes did die.

THIRD PERSON: (Eagle) Our bird is called the Bald Eagle; his power is might and regal; within our fair land; his emblem does stand; his seal is on all that is legal.

FOURTH PERSON: (Liberty Bell) We treasure our Liberty Bell; freedom news, long ago it did tell; our Independence Declaration; it told to our nation;

as it peeled out the news "All is well."

FIFTH PERSON: (Capital) Americans love the fair sight; of the capitol dome, gleaming white; her men pass the laws; to spread freedom's cause; and guard against tyranny's blight.

SIXTH PERSON: (Uncle Sam) Should Uncle Sam beckon you; to serve on his Liberty crew; then try with your might; to help win the fight; for freedom, to pay what is due.

SEVENTH PERSON: (Star Spangled Banner song) The Star Spangled Banner is our song; to Americans it will always belong; long may she wave; over the home of the brave; these words we'll sing proudly and long.

ANNOUNCER: We are fifty states, all in all; whose standards never shall fall; our motto is just; in God we do trust; freedom, if you need us, just call.

BALLOON MADNESS

SETTING: Two people are needed to come in and do speaking parts. Have lots of balloons and a small pin for each person. There also need to be several other people to blow up and pop balloons.
SCENE: The people are on stage blowing up balloons to full size then popping the balloon with pins. (Do not have to tie ends.) Continue with other balloons until the skit is over. Let the people blow and pop several balloons before the two with speaking parts come in.

FIRST PERSON: What are they doing?

SECOND PERSON: Blowing up balloons then popping them.

FIRST PERSON: Why?

SECOND PERSON: It is a contest.

FIRST PERSON: Oh, what does the winner get?

SECOND PERSON: Nothing.

FIRST PERSON: Well, then what does the loser get?

It's Showtime!

SECOND PERSON: He will have to buy the bags of balloons for the next contest!

HILLBILLY FAMILY

SETTING: Five or more people are needed to be part of the family and one person to do the sound effects.
SCENE: The Hillbilly family is all laying around on the floor with straw or hay in their mouth. They hear a howl in the distance off stage. People should speak very slowly like a country hillbilly family.

FIRST PERSON: Hey, (name of person), will you see who it is?

SECOND PERSON: I'm just too tired to move. Hey, (name of person), will you see who it is?

THIRD PERSON: I'm just too tired to move. Hey, (name of person), will you see who it is?

FOURTH PERSON: I'm just too tired to move. Hey, (name of person), will you see who it is?

(This continues until all the people on floor have done it. Finally, one designated person gets up and goes off stage for just a second. He then returns and lays back down on the floor.)

FIRST PERSON: What was it?

DESIGNATED PERSON: It was a coyote, sittin' on a cactus, howling. He was just too tired to move!

PEACE BE WITH YOU

SETTING: Seven people with one selected to be the Chief and other six to be Indians.
SCENE: Have them dressed in war paint and simple Indian costumes, gathered around a campfire.

CHIEF: (Talking very slowly.) I have called this council meeting to decide if we make peace with the white man.

FIRST BRAVE: They take away our land many moons ago. I say no peace.

SECOND BRAVE: They not smoke peace pipe with us. I say no peace.

THIRD BRAVE: Their fire water, not good medicine. I say no peace.

FOURTH BRAVE: They copy our customs and use more powerful weapons. I say no peace.

FIFTH BRAVE: They take the blue from the sky and the gold from the sun. I say no peace.

SIXTH BRAVE: I say let the Chief decide.

CHIEF: You all speak the truth. But some of white man's medicine is much good. When they take our customs, colors from sky and sun of blue and gold, it is used to help make them good scouts. Perhaps peace not far away.

ALL ABOARD

SETTING: Six are needed for speaking parts with one assigned as the conductor. Have as many other people as you like. Have a train depot setting with chairs around in two or three lines and an "EXIT" door. The person assigned to be the conductor is dressed with a blue overcoat and a railroad type hat. He can also carry a clipboard.

SCENE: Several people sitting around, reading a book or newspaper, some can pretend to be napping, others can just be looking around. In walks the conductor. People walk up one at a time.

CONDUCTOR: (Speaking in a loud voice.) All aboard: Last call for trip number 312. All aboard!

FIRST PERSON: (Walks up to conductor.) Excuse me sir, are you sure this train is going to stop in Dallas, Texas?

CONDUCTOR: We're sure gonna try! (Person walks through train depot door.)

SECOND PERSON: (Walks up to conductor.) Excuse me sir, are you sure this train is going to stop in Albuquerque, New Mexico?

It's Showtime!

CONDUCTOR: We're sure gonna try! (Person walks through train depot door.)

THIRD PERSON: (Walks up to conductor.) Excuse me sir, are you sure this train is going to stop in Phoenix, Arizona?

CONDUCTOR: We're sure gonna try! (Person walks through train depot door.)

FOURTH PERSON: (Walks up to conductor.) Excuse me sir, are you sure this train is going to stop in Las Vegas, Nevada?

CONDUCTOR: We're sure gonna try! (Person walks through train depot door.)

FIFTH PERSON: (Walks up to conductor.) Excuse me sir, are you sure this train is going to stop in San Francisco, California?

CONDUCTOR: Well, if we don't, I hope everyone can swim 'cause there's gonna be one great big SPLASH!

BAKED ALASKA

SETTING: Five people selected to do speaking parts then as many other people as you like. You need a table that has cooking supplies on it—sugar, bowls, cups, spoons, flour, salt, pepper, etc. Have as many as possible wearing aprons as though they are chefs. Have a large cookbook on hand, have it propped up if you can. Have a glass of water offstage.
SCENE: Four people gathered around the table as cooks pretend to be reading, mixing, and talking. In comes the first speaker.

FIRST PERSON: Hey all! What are you up to?

SECOND PERSON: We have been studying about Alaska.

FIRST PERSON: (Looking pleased.) Oh yea?! Great! Well, what have you done here? (Pointing to the things on the table.)

SECOND PERSON: We have just made a "Baked Alaska."

THIRD PERSON: And it's cooking now.

FIRST PERSON: A "Baked Alaska" is not easy to do. I'm impressed! Well, how much longer will it take to cook?

FOURTH PERSON: It should just about be ready. I'll go and see. (He goes off stage and returns with a glass of water and hands it to the First Person.)

FIRST PERSON: (Looking puzzled.) Well, that was nice, but I'm not thirsty. I would rather see your "Baked Alaska".

SECOND PERSON: We read that Alaska has ice and snow all over the place.

THIRD PERSON: Yea. So we looked up Alaska in this cookbook (points to book) and found "Baked Alaska".

FOURTH PERSON: We figured that if you take some ice and shave it up, it would be the same as snow. So we got some ice cubes and shaved them up into a glass.

SECOND PERSON: Then we baked it at 400 degrees for about 15 minutes and now we have a "Baked Alaska!"

(First Person holds up the water and all the people point to the glass and smile.)

THE LIBERTY BELL

SETTING: Seven people for speaking parts with one selected to be the announcer. Six people will need half sheets of poster board with the dates from the skit on the front and the words on the back. Have a big poster with the Liberty Bell drawn on it.
SCENE: Have the Liberty Bell poster propped up in a chair. All people are

It's Showtime!

gathered around the bell with their posters. As it's their turn, they should read about each date.

ANNOUNCER: One of the most cherished symbols of American Independence is the famous Liberty Bell, now preserved in a special building in Philadelphia. It has been rung on a number of important occasions. some of which we'd like to tell you about.

FIRST PERSON: On July 4, 1776, the bell was rung to announce the official adoption of the Declaration of Independence. This was actually the birthday of our nation, and marks the most important single event in our history.

SECOND PERSON: On October 14, 1781, it was rung to celebrate the surrender of Lord Cornwallis of the English forces and the virtual ending of the Revolutionary War. On April 6, 1783, it announced the proclamation of peace with Great Britain.

THIRD PERSON: On September 29, 1824, it was rung to welcome Lafayette, the famous French general who had assisted Washington, to Independence Hall. On July 4, 1826, it tolled to announce the death of Thomas Jefferson, principal author of the Declaration of Independence.

FOURTH PERSON: On July 14, 1826, it ushered in "The Year of Jubilee," the 50th Anniversary of the American Republic. On July 4, 1831, the famous bell rang for the last time on Independence Day.

FIFTH PERSON: On February 22, 1832, the bell was rung to commemorate the birthday of George Washington. Later that same year it tolled to announce the death of the last surviving signer of the Declaration of Independence, Charles Carroll of Carrollton, Georgia.

SIXTH PERSON: On July 8, 1835, while it was being tolled for the death of Chief Justice John Marshall, a crack developed in the bell. It started from the brim and inclined in a right hand direction toward the crown. On February 22, 1843, when an attempt was being made to ring the bell on Washington's birthday, the fracture increased to such an extent that no effort has been made to ring it since that time.

ANNOUNCER: Some of you may have been to Philadelphia to see the Liberty Bell. Perhaps you remember the inscription "PROCLAIM LIBERTY

THROUGHOUT THE LAND," from which the bell got it's name.

ON THE LINE

SETTING: Two people are needed for the skit with the help of the audience.
SCENE: Use a tin can telephone with about 30 feet of heavy colored line that can be seen by the audience. People should station themselves at each end of the telephone with the line pulled tight just off the floor.

FIRST PERSON: Hello, (name of person). Can you hear me?

SECOND PERSON: What did you say?

(The First Person asks two children from the audience to help hold the line up over their head)

FIRST PERSON: (Name of person), can you hear me now?

SECOND PERSON: I can barely hear you. Speak up!

(First Person asks a few more children and an adult or two to help hold the line up)

FIRST PERSON: (Name of Person), am I coming through any clearer now?

SECOND PERSON: That is a little better, but you still need to speak up.

(First Person gets tall adults to hold the line up.)

FIRST PERSON: (Name of Person), can you hear me now?

SECOND PERSON: I can hear you just fine now, but there seems to be a lot of static. I think we must have a whole nest of squirrels sitting "on the line."

EXTRA, EXTRA!

SETTING: Two people are needed for speaking parts, a paperboy and a man. Other people are standing around reading.
SCENE: Paperboy with other people around newspaper stand.

It's Showtime!

PAPERBOY: Extra! Extra! Read all about it! Great mystery! Fifty victims. Extra! Extra! (In walks man.) Paper, mister?

MAN: Yes, I'll buy one. (Gives him money and gets paper.)

PAPERBOY: Extra! Extra! Read all about it! Great mystery! Fifty-One victims. Extra! Extra! (Man looks at his paper bewildered.)

GENERAL CUSTER

SETTING: One person selected to be General Custer and one selected to be the Solider. A few other soldiers and a few Indians are needed. One arrow with a note attached will be needed as a prop.
SCENE: Indians on stage sitting in a circle.

(General Custer charges in with boys yelling, "Bang, Bang" as if shooting their guns. Indians get up as if to get their weapons. One by one all men and Indians are shot down. The last Solider beside Custer gets shot with an arrow that has a note on it. Suggestion; have the arrow sitting on the side and the Solider picks it up and puts it under his arm as if shot.)

SOLIDER: Wait, wait, there's a note on it. (Takes off and reads it.)

CUSTER: What does it say?

SOLIDER: It's for you. (The solider takes the arrow out of himself and stabs it in Custer and then walks off.)

BEACH BUMMER

SETTING: Two people are needed for speaking parts and at least three other people. They should dress in swimsuits and have a blanket and picnic supplies on hand. Have a pitcher, lemonade package, plates, cups, napkins, and even some food if you can.
SCENE: Have blanket and picnic supplies on stage ahead of time. People then come in and lay around the blanket.

FIRST PERSON: Boy, today at the beach has been great! Let's get started with lunch. (Ask each person to do a task and then work on that task.)

(Name of person), I need you to get the plates and pass them out.
(Name of person), will you get the cups and pass them out.
(Name of person-this will be "Second Person" later on), will you make the lemonade for us? (This person goes off stage with the package of lemonade.)
(Name of person), will you get the sandwich fixings and put them on the blanket.
O.K. everyone, lets start making our sandwiches.
(In walks the person with the opened package of lemonade and goes up to the first person.)

SECOND PERSON: I'm having some problems.

FIRST PERSON: Like what?

SECOND PERSON: Well, after reading the directions, I'm having a hard time getting eight cups of water into this package!

PUMPKIN PIE PATCH

SETTING: Fourteen people are needed for speaking parts and as many others as you want. (Or eight people each responsible for two parts.) Twelve (or six) people need to be dressed as pumpkins. Costumes can be cut from orange poster boards and simple held up to the body. The people need to be able to sit or squat on the floor. Two need to be dressed as a mother and child. Each pumpkin needs a small sign that reads "The End" and one sign is needed to say "Pumpkin Patch."
SCENE: Have pumpkins sitting in the pumpkin patch with their signs on the floor out of sight. Have the "Pumpkin Patch" sign propped up.

FIRST PERSON: (Angrily.) Well, here we are in the patch once again. I hate being a pumpkin.

SECOND PERSON: I know what you mean. Pretty soon they'll all be over here, poking and squeezing and trying to decide how to dress us up.

It's Showtime!

THIRD PERSON: (Loudly.) I'm tired of being carved! It hurts!

FOURTH PERSON: (Smiling.) I wish they'd give me a pretty smile and not tooth decay.

FIFTH PERSON: (Wiping his brow.) And that candle gets so hot. Boy, were they glad I used Dial!

SIXTH PERSON: Well, it's better than crayon all over your face. They really get carried away. I even had a beard and mustache.

SEVENTH PERSON: Be thankful for a beard and mustache. How would you like to be wearing a girl's wig? I was humiliated!

EIGHTH PERSON: At least a wig is soft. The family I was with stuck gourds all over my head. Two ears, two eyes and a big nose!

NINTH PERSON: I keep getting a spot on the window sill. I need more room than that. You can't imagine the bruises I have from falling.

TENTH PERSON: Well, I resent when they decide to build a pyramid with two or three of us. They call it a "pumpkin man!" I call it sore shoulders!

ELEVENTH PERSON: I've been listening to you all complain for the last ten minutes, and not one of you has mentioned being put outside. Every year for one solid week, I get the place of honor on the front porch.

TWELFTH PERSON: Me too! The least they could do is take us in when it rains, or give us a raincoat.

(Mother and child come in and start looking at the pumpkins.)

FIRST PERSON: (Pointing to the family coming up.) Be quiet! Here they come. Maybe we'll be too small or the wrong shape.

CHILD: (Excited.) Mommy, over here. Lots of pumpkins!

MOTHER: Why, these pumpkins are too small and some are all twisted out of shape. We need to keep looking for that right pumpkin.

ALL PUMPKINS: Thank goodness!

MOTHER: (Very slowing says as she is eyeing each pumpkin.) But....they'll make perfect.... PUMPKIN PIES!

ALL PUMPKINS: (Groan in unison.) Oh, no! (Hold up their signs... "The End")

BROKEN LAWNMOWER

SETTING: One person will pretend he is the lawnmower and be positioned on his hands and knees. Use as many other people as you want. Plan ahead on going out into the audience and getting one person to come up and help you with the lawnmower. (Generally this is an unsuspecting dad or host of the party. Someone who can take a joke.)
SCENE: Have the person who is the lawnmower in the center of the stage on his hands and knees. The other people enter one at a time to try to start the lawnmower.

FIRST PERSON: (He enters and try's to pull start the lawnmower. The lawnmower just gives a few spurts and dies out.)

SECOND PERSON: (Enters.) What are you doing?

FIRST PERSON: I am trying to start the lawnmower. I can't seem to do it. Will you try?

SECOND PERSON: Sure. (All he gets are a few spurts.) Maybe the spark plug is loose. (He checks.)

THIRD PERSON: (Enters.) Hi, guys. What's up?

FIRST PERSON: We can't seem to start the mower. Will you try?

THIRD PERSON: Yea. (He tries and gets nothing.) Is there plenty of gas? (He checks.)

(Continue in this manner until all people have tried to start the mower. The lawnmower never starts, although it does try several times, but just dies back out. After all have tried, the first person speaks...)

It's Showtime!

FIRST PERSON: Well, it seems we are just not strong enough to do it. We need some help. (He looks out into the audience and looks at the person you have decided to get ahead of time—this person does not know he is to take part in your skit, it is a surprise to him/her.)

FIRST PERSON: I know who we can get. (Go and get that person and bring him up on stage.) Please try to start our lawnmower.

(The special person gives the lawnmower a pull and the lawnmower starts.)

FIRST PERSON: That's great! All we needed was a big "JERK!"

HIGHER COURT

This is a three part skit or a run-on. Do each part at different times throughout the program.

SETTING: One person is selected to be holding a suitcase and one to do a speaking part. You will need a small ladder, or if no ladder is available just hold your suitcase over your head. The host of the program can do the speaking part of the first person or assign the job.
SCENE: The second person enters the room at different times to get the effect of the run-on. In comes the person with the suitcase.

(Part One)
FIRST PERSON: (Host or designated person.) Where are you going?

SECOND PERSON: (Carrying suitcase, pauses to answer.) I'm taking my case to court.

(Part Two - Second Person now has a suitcase and small ladder.)
FIRST PERSON: Where are you going now?

SECOND PERSON: I'm taking my case to a higher court.

(Part Three - Second Person is carrying nothing.)
FIRST PERSON: What happened?

SECOND PERSON: I lost my case!

CHRISTMAS CAROLS

SETTING: Six people are needed with one selected as Santa and one selected as Mom. A small sign that reads "The End" is pinned to the bottom of the fourth person and the audience does not see it until the end.
SCENE: Santa and Mom are off stage. The other people are at center stage talking to each other.

FIRST PERSON: Boy, (Looking around.) it looks like it's going to be a *White Christmas* after all. Say, do you hear *Jingle Bells*?

SECOND PERSON: No, that's *Silent Night*. Maybe you heard *Rudolph the Red Nosed Reindeer.*

THIRD PERSON: I bet he heard *Frosty the Snowman* out walking in a *Winter Wonderland.*

FIRST PERSON: Boy, I can hardly wait until morning cause *Santa Claus is Comin' to Town!* What do you want (name of person)?

SECOND PERSON: Well, *All I Want for Christmas* is a hippopotamus, but I don't know if Santa can take him for a *Sleigh Ride.*

THIRD PERSON: Mom will love that! *All I Want for Christmas is My Two Front Teeth!*

FIRST PERSON: I want a *Little Drummer Boy*, some *Silver Bells* and *Away in the Manger.*

FOURTH PERSON: (Looking a little sad.) Gee, I bet *I'm Getting Nuthin' for Christmas* because *I Saw Mommy Kissing Santa Claus.* Besides, I hit *Wee Three Kings* with a *Jingle Bell Rock.*

SECOND PERSON: Oh, oh, it's gonna be a *Blue Christmas* for (name of fourth person).

THIRD PERSON: That's O.K. (name of person), this is going to be the best *Joy to the World*, and I will share my toys with you.

It's Showtime!

MOTHER: (Off stage.) Hey, it's time for bed! Remember, *Santa Claus is Coming to Town!*

ALL: (Scramble around and whisper to each other then yell...) Yes mother! (All come forward, stand in a line, face audience and ask them to join you in singing... *We Wish You a Merry Christmas.*)

(Offstage you hear bells jingling.)
SANTA: (Offstage, and singing the first couple of lines to...) *Here Comes Santa Claus*, here comes Santa Claus, right down Santa Claus lane.

(People run off stage except fourth person. He turns around so that the audience can see the "THE END" sign. Then he runs off.)

VINDOW VIPER

SETTING: Four people are needed for speaking parts.
SCENE: Have each person come running in just a few seconds behind the one before.

FIRST PERSON: (Comes running in and yelling.) The Viper is coming! The Viper is coming! (Runs off stage.)

SECOND PERSON: (Comes running in and yelling.) The Viper is coming! The Viper is coming! (Runs off stage.)

THIRD PERSON: (Comes running in and yelling.) The Viper is coming! The Viper is coming! (Runs off stage.)

FOURTH PERSON: (Comes strolling in leisurely, carrying a rag and a pail.) Hello, I'm the Vindow Viper, can I do your vindows?

WRONG FEET

SETTING: One person with his shoes on the wrong feet. Four others are needed for speaking parts.
SCENE: Person with shoes on wrong feet in center of stage with a painful expression on face. Other people enter one at a time.

SECOND PERSON: (Enters looking at first person.) What's wrong?

FIRST PERSON: My feet are killing me!

SECOND PERSON: Do you have corns on your feet?

FIRST PERSON: No.

THIRD PERSON: (Enters looking at first person.) What's wrong?

FIRST PERSON: My feet are killing me?

THIRD PERSON: Do you have bunions?

FIRST PERSON: No.

FOURTH PERSON: (Enters looking at first person.) What's wrong?

FIRST PERSON: My feet are killing me!

FOURTH PERSON: Have you been walking a lot?

FIRST PERSON: No.

FIFTH PERSON: (Enters looking at first person.) What's wrong?

FIRST PERSON: My feet are killing me!

FIFTH PERSON: (Looks down at first person's feet.) Oh, I see. You have your shoes on the wrong feet!

FIRST PERSON: (Looks at fifth person rather exasperated.) Well, they are the *only* feet I have!

JELLY BEANS

SETTING: One person selected to be the storekeeper. They should wear an apron and old glasses. At least four other people are needed for speaking parts. A table, feather duster, a tin or plastic container labeled "Jelly Beans," a small ladder, and a shelf.

It's Showtime!

SCENE: In the center of the stage, the storekeeper is standing behind the counter (table) dusting the counter. Behind the counter is the shelf with the jar of jelly beans in it and the ladder in front of it. First person enters and walks up to the counter.

STOREKEEPER: May I help you?

FIRST PERSON: I would like ten cents worth of jelly beans, please.

(Storekeeper walks back to ladder, climbs it, gets container, climbs down, sets the container on the counter, removes lid, counts out ten jelly beans. He puts lid back on container, climbs back up ladder to replace container and climbs down, returns to the counter.)

STOREKEEPER: That will be ten cents please.

FIRST PERSON: (Counts out ten cents and takes jelly beans.) Thank you. (Leaves.)

(Enters second person.)
STOREKEEPER: May I help you?

SECOND PERSON: I would like ten cents worth of jelly beans, please.

(Storekeeper walks back to ladder, climbs it, gets container, climbs down, sets the container on the counter, removes lid, counts out ten jelly beans. He puts lid back on container, climbs back up ladder to replace container and climbs down, returns to the counter.)

STOREKEEPER: That will be ten cents please.

SECOND PERSON: (Counts out ten cents and takes jelly beans.) Thank you. (Leaves.)

(Enters third person.)
STOREKEEPER: May I help you?

THIRD PERSON: I would like ten cents worth of jelly beans, please.

(Storekeeper walks back to ladder, climbs it, gets container, climbs down, sets the container on the counter, removes lid, counts out ten jelly beans, puts lid back on container, but this time leaves the container on the counter.)

STOREKEEPER: That will be ten cents please.

THIRD PERSON: (Counts out ten cents and takes jelly beans.) Thank you. (Leaves.)

(Enters fourth person.)
STOREKEEPER: (In a rather confident voice.) Don't tell me! I know what you want. Your want ten cents worth of jelly beans. (Takes lid off container.)

FOURTH PERSON: No sir, I don't want ten cents worth of jelly beans.

STOREKEEPER: You don't! (Looks surprised.)

FOURTH PERSON: No, sir.

STOREKEEPER: Are you sure you don't want ten cents worth of jelly beans?

FOURTH PERSON: Yes sir, I'm sure.

STOREKEEPER: Thank goodness! Just a minute. (He replaces the lid and returns the container to the top of the shelf and returns to the counter.) Well then, what can I do for you?

FOURTH PERSON: I would like 15 cents worth of jelly beans, please!

A FOOL'S GOLD

SETTING: Five people are needed with one selected as an old prospector and one as a pirate.
SCENE: A blue tarp is needed for the creek, gold nuggets (spray painted rocks) are scattered up and down the creek. Have tarp wrinkled a little to hide the nuggets. Prospector has a pie pan and is pretending to pan for gold. The pirate is off stage out of sight. The three people come in.

FIRST PERSON: What are you doing?

It's Showtime!

PROSPECTOR: (Crustily.) What do you think I'm doing?

SECOND PERSON: Looks like you're playing in the water.

PROSPECTOR: Well I'm not. I'm panning for gold.

THIRD PERSON: (Excited.) Can we try?

PROSPECTOR: Well, I don't know. You look like a bunch of ding-dang fools to me!

FIRST PERSON: No were not, please let us try!

PROSPECTOR: Well, I guess it's O.K..

(Prospector hands the first person his pan. He dips it in the water a couple of times and comes up with a piece of gold. He then hands the pan to the second person, who moves down stream just a little and does the same. He then hands it to the third person who moves a little down stream and he does the same. They should gently pick up a gold nugget when they are panning.)

FIRST PERSON: We sure do thank you for letting us pan in your stream.

PROSPECTOR: Yeah, sure. Just don't be a fool and tell everyone where you got it. Another thing, don't go around showing it off!

(The people thank him and walk away talking about their nuggets. A pirate jumps out into their path and the people try to hide their nuggets.)

PIRATE: Give me all your gold! Don't tell me you don't have any, I saw you get it!

(The people argue a little but the Pirate insists. They soon hand it over and the pirate leaves.)

SECOND PERSON: Oh well, that just goes to show you. A fool and his gold are soon pirated.

CONFUSED DRUMMER

SETTING: Three people are selected for parts. One person is dressed as an Indian drummer with drum and tom-tom. Another person is the guide for the tour and one other is selected from those on the tour. There can be as many other people as you want. As the Indian drummer beats out his messages, try to vary the style and speed of the drumming to represent different messages.

SCENE: Indian is seated on the floor with drum and tom-toms. The tour guide and guests enter from the other side of stage.

TOUR GUIDE: This is the tribe's drummer. His name is Smoking Eagle. He is named that because he can translate all messages that come in to the tribe. It can be smoke signals, Indian writing messages, or drum messages.

(Indian drummer beats out a short message.)

TOUR GUIDE: He says there is going to be a meeting of the council tonight and that you are invited.

(Indian drummer beats out a short message.)

TOUR GUIDE: He says there will be good food and dancing.

(Indian drummer beats out a short message.)

TOUR GUIDE: He says that many of the braves will be honored for a good hunt.

(Indian drummer beats out a short message.)

TOUR GUIDE: He says that the Chief will give blessings to the god's for a successful hunt.

(Indian drummer beats out a short message.)

(This time the Tour Guide looks puzzled. The guests shake their head in confusion.)

It's Showtime!

(Indian drummer beats out the same message again.)

(Tour Guide and guests still look confused.)

(Indian drummer beats out the message for the third time.)

GUEST: (Excited and somewhat yelling.) I got it! Smoking Eagle says to telephone him if there's anything we want him to bring to the meeting!

TOUR GUIDE: (Disgustedly.) Telephone him!

(Guests walk off and leave Tour Guide and Indian drummer looking at each other confused.)

MANY MUSCLES

SETTING: Seven people are needed with one being dressed as a beautiful curvy girl. All other people wear shorts over pants to resemble sweat suits except one who is in regular clothes. You will need jump rope, dumbbells, and barbells.

SCENE: People in shorts are on stage doing various exercises. Jumping rope, doing sit-ups, jumping jacks, lifting barbells, and dumbbells. In walks person in regular clothes who goes to different people exercising.

FIRST PERSON: Why are you doing this?

SECOND PERSON: Because I like many muscles.

FIRST PERSON: Why are you doing this?

THIRD PERSON: Because I like many muscles.

FIRST PERSON: Why are you doing this?

FOURTH PERSON: Because I like many muscles.

FIRST PERSON: Why are you doing this?

FIFTH PERSON: Because I like many muscles.

(Person dressed as girl comes in over to first person.)

FIRST PERSON: Who are you?

GIRL: Why, I am Minnie Muscles!

(All people follow her off stage.)

I AM AN AMERICAN

SETTING: Twelve people are needed.
SCENE: Everyone will be standing on stage in a straight line with, their lines written on index cards. When it's their time to talk, they take a step forward, read lines, then step back. This is an appropriate prelude to the Pledge of Allegiance.

FIRST PERSON: My country gives each one of us the opportunity to advance according to his ambition. Education is for all. I am an America.

SECOND PERSON: My country means love of freedom, faith in democracy, justice, and equality. I am an American.

THIRD PERSON: My country believes in the moral worth of the common man. I am an American.

FOURTH PERSON: My country gives us the privilege of expressing beliefs or opinions without fear of persecution. I am an American.

FIFTH PERSON: My country has the best form of government. It is our duty to keep it that way. I am an American.

SIXTH PERSON: My country promises life, liberty, and the pursuit of happiness. I am an American.

SEVENTH PERSON: My country gives us a privilege that we shall protect and defend even with our lives. I am an American.

EIGHTH PERSON: My country is and always shall remain the land of the free and the home of the brave. I am an American.

NINTH PERSON: My country offers a living Americanism which demands an informed, intelligent, and active citizenship. I am an American.

TENTH PERSON: My country meets any needs or suffering with its abiding love and loyalty. I am an American.

ELEVENTH PERSON: My country is the servant....not the master. I am an American.

TWELFTH PERSON: My country possesses a Statue of Liberty whose torch shall burn as long as we keep it alight with our devotion to the freedom of the individual. I am an American.

SOME BEACH

SETTING: Four people are needed for speaking parts with as many others as you like. Have one person dressed as a cowboy with hat and boots. Have others dressed in swimsuits with towels and sunglasses. Make a cactus out of cardboard.
SCENE: The cowboy is on stage leaning up against the cactus. He is laid back, taking it easy, fanning himself with his hat. Enter the other people.

COWBOY: Say, where do you think you're going?

FIRST PERSON: Why, swimming of course.

COWBOY: But this is the Sahara Desert!

SECOND PERSON: Oh really? (Looking around.)

COWBOY: You are more than 100 miles from the sea!

THIRD PERSON: Boy, some beach front! Come on, this won't take too much longer. (People walk off stage.)

WELCOME TO OUR NEIGHBORHOOD

SETTING: As many as ten people are needed with one selected to be the announcer. Try to have a recording of "Mister Rogers Neighborhood" playing in the background. Turn it down when the people start to speak. You will need hats for each part for them to wear or have the hats on a table so they can come up and pick them up.

SCENE: People come on stage wearing hats (or pick them up off table when their turn to speak). One at a time people turn to the audience and tell them about that hat, using hand motions to help explain what they are saying. They then go to side of stage. Announcer sets the scene with opening and closing.

ANNOUNCER: Welcome to our neighborhood. Today I want to introduce you to some of the people who you might find in your neighborhood. (Move to back side of stage.)

FIRST PERSON: (Cowboy hat) I am a Cowboy– Round them up, tie them up, wagons ho! Round them up, tie them up. wagons ho!

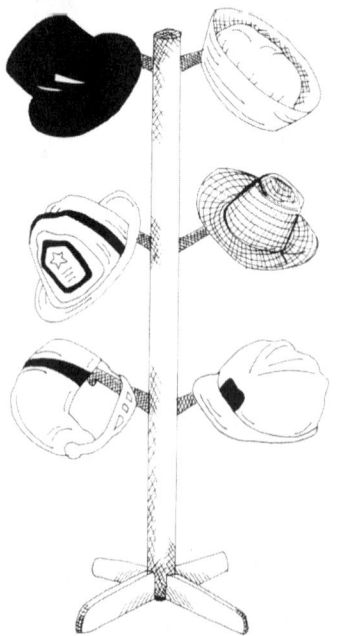

SECOND PERSON: (Fireman hat) I am a Fireman–I'll take the hose, this way men! I'll take the hose, this way men!

THIRD PERSON: (Chef hat) I am a Baker–Sweets for sale! Sweets for sale!

FOURTH PERSON: (Sombrero) I am a Spanish Dancer–La Cucaracha, La Cucaracha!

FIFTH PERSON: (Policeman hat) I am a Policeman–Stop, go this way, please! Stop, go this way, please!

SIXTH PERSON: (Top hat) I am a Magician–Abracadabra! Abracadabra!

SEVENTH PERSON: (Baseball hat) I am a

It's Showtime!

Baseball Player–I hit a home run! I hit a home run!

EIGHTH PERSON: (Hard hat) I am a Construction Worker–Watch out! People working! Watch out! People working!

NINTH PERSON: (Football helmet) I am a Football Player–I'm in for the touchdown! I'm in for the touchdown!

ANNOUNCER: Explore your neighborhood today and see who lives there.

THIS IS YOUR LIFE

PLEASE NOTE: Do a little research on your own state. Look through an encyclopedia for information like; when did it join the Union, the nickname, from where the name was derived, what is it's major industry, the state symbols, a date in history that is prominent for your state, a famous person from your state and others. Using that information, you will need that number of people to present this skit. For the purpose of showing the skit, we will honor the state of Texas.

SETTING: One person has a cardboard cut out of the state strapped over his shoulders. Be sure it is large enough to be seen from the stage. One person is the announcer and carries with him a make–believe microphone. Use as many other people as you have information. I suggest using 10 to 12 extra people so the skit will be interesting and informative. Others can be standing around for support.

SCENE: On stage is the announcer and all the people, except your state person. They pretend to be talking among themselves. Enters "YOUR STATE" looking surprised.

ANNOUNCER: (As "Texas" enters, speak into the mic.) And here is our guest of honor! Texas, This Is Your Life! (Texas is very surprised as he looks around. Other people clap and cheer.)

ANNOUNCER: (Play the part of host, put your arm around Texas and refer to him off and on during the skit.) I know this is a surprise to you! Today we honor our very special friend and state, Texas. We know so many special points about you! So let's get started so others will know more about you, too! (Have each person approach "Texas" as it is time for him to speak.)

FIRST PERSON: I know all about your name! The Spanish named you after the first mission that they established in 1689 called "San Francisco de Los Tejas," Tejas is an Indian word that means "Friends."

SECOND PERSON: And your nickname is "The Lone Star State."

ANNOUNCER: And that's not all! We also know what kind of mileage you have!

THIRD PERSON: Your total area is over 267,000 square miles. You are the second largest of all states.

FOURTH PERSON: Your state capital is Austin and Houston is the most populated city with about at two million people.

ANNOUNCER: You surely have grown to be very big. Not only in size, but in manufacturing.

FIFTH PERSON: Petroleum refining is still one of your major industries, but the largest is the manufacture of chemicals.

SIXTH PERSON: Houston is not only your largest city, but it holds the record for having the largest ship channel ever. The Houston Ship Channel is 50 miles long.

ANNOUNCER: Like other states of the Union you have selected state symbols.

SEVENTH PERSON: Your state flower is the Bluebonnet and your state tree is the Pecan Tree.

EIGHTH PERSON: The Mockingbird is your state bird and your shrimp catch is the nation's largest.

NINTH PERSON: The Comanches Indians were perhaps the most dominant during the 17th and 18th century.

ANNOUNCER: Now comes the most important years of your life! Tell us all about it (as he points to the next person).

TENTH PERSON: After the capture of Santa Anna in 1836, Texas was final-

It's Showtime!

ly free from Mexico and declared itself as a Republic. The Republic of Texas tried several times to have their country annexed by the United States, but failed.

ELEVENTH PERSON: It was sought by President Tyler (1841-45) and was advocated by James K. Polk during the 1844 Presidential campaign. After Polk was elected, but while Tyler was still in office, Congress passed a joint resolution authorizing annexation. Statehood was approved on December 29, 1845, making you the 28th state in the Union. Unlike other new states, which first became a territory, Texas was admitted directly.

ANNOUNCER: We are proud of you "Texas!" Now others know a little bit more about how wonderful you really are. Because, This Is Your Life!

(Everyone clap and cheer and gather around Texas.)

THE FORGOTTEN TREASURE

SETTING: Six people are needed all dressed as pirates. Make the side view of a pirate ship and prop up using chairs. After deciding who will be who, get the props needed to portray that person.
SCENE: The ship is on stage with the pirates on board the ship (just standing behind it).

LOOKOUT: Land Ho! Off the port bow!

CAPTAIN: Well men, it shouldn't be long now.

FIRST MATE: Yes sir! Soon we will once again touch our precious treasure.

SHIP OFFICER: Remember the ruby and diamond necklace? That will be enough for me to live on comfortably.

CREW MAN: I would be happy with the rings of gold.

COOK: With the gold coins, I could have someone else cook for me.

CAPTAIN: We've docked, men. Let's go! (They disembark the ship....each going in a different direction.)

CAPTAIN: Men, where are you going?

FIRST MATE: To the treasure, it's this way! (Points in a direction.)

COOK: No, man, it's this way! (Points in another direction.)

CREW MEMBER: No, no! It's over here! (Points in another direction.)

SHIP OFFICER: No, you fool, it's back here! (Points in another direction.)

LOOKOUT: Oh No! We forgot where we buried the treasure!

CHRISTMAS AROUND THE WORLD

SETTING: Eight people are needed. Each person will need half sheets of poster board that show what the country he is talking about does at Christmas. Example: If you are England, your poster will have cards on it.
SCENE: Have each person in a line with posters up so everyone can see. Have written on the back what they are to say.

FIRST PERSON: England was the first country to use the Christmas card. This started over 100 years ago.

SECOND PERSON: In France, a "Cake of The Kings" is made. On January 6th, the Three Kings are placed around the manger of the baby Jesus. In making the cake, a single bean is placed in the batter. The person finding it is given a crown and becomes the king of the party.

THIRD PERSON: The Tannenbaum, or Christmas Tree, comes from Germany. A minister saw a little pine tree covered with fresh snow, glistening in the moonlight. He thought the tree would be beautiful if it was decorated and inside the house. For many years the German people lighted their trees with waxed candles of various colors. They also hung cookies and fresh fruits on its branches.

FOURTH PERSON: Christmas comes before December 5th in Holland. Saint Nicholas comes sailing into the harbor of many Dutch cities. He brings his white horse and his companion "Black Pete." The children get ready for this visit by putting their wooden shoes outside their door. They fill them with carrots and hay for Santa's horse and the next day the children find surprises that Saint Nicholas left.

FIFTH PERSON: In Italy, each family has a miniature model of the Nativity.

It's Showtime!

The day before Christmas the family fasts until evening. They gather around the fire at night and presents are exchanged in a big jar called the "Urn o Fate." On January 6th, the good witch, Le Befana comes to the children. She leaves ashes in the shoes of the children who have not been good and presents for those who have been good.

SIXTH PERSON: In Mexico, the holidays begin on December 6th. Then a nine day "posada" starts which shows the procession that Mary and Joseph took looking for a room in the inn before baby Jesus was born. The family carries a statue but the infant baby Jesus is not placed in the manger until Christmas Eve. Everyone parties with piñatas and poinsettias on Christmas day. Gift giving does not come until January 6th. That is when Saint Nicholas comes.

SEVENTH PERSON: The oldest daughter plays the role of Saint Lucia in Sweden and serves sweet rolls and coffee to the family. She wears a lighted advent wreath on her head and sings carols. On Christmas Eve, the family gathers in the kitchen and dips a piece of black bread in hot broth, this is to bring them good luck in the coming year. A small elf-like figure, Juletamte, brings the gifts. He puts them on the floor and then leaves. Then the family enjoys a large supper.

EIGHTH PERSON: In America, we enjoy a little of all the customs of the world. Our Christmas trees are brightly decorated with lights and ornaments. We enjoy big banquets over Christmas Eve and Christmas Day. We exchange gifts of toys among children and Santa Claus visits the homes of children on Christmas Eve. This is a time of love, laughter and good cheer.

GOD BLESS AMERICA

SETTING: Sixteen people are needed with one being selected to be the announcer. Or use eight people and let each be responsible for two parts. You will need half sheets of poster board with these letters written big: G, O, D, B, L, E, S, S, A, M, E, R, I, C, A. On the back of each have the following skit written.

SCENE: People come on stage in the letter order and one at a time hold up their posters and read what is on the back. They should not lower their letter when done, it should stay raised. When done, the announcer will ask everyone to rise and join in on this song.

FIRST PERSON: (Hold up "G") Irving Berlin came to America when he was four years old when his family fled Russia.

(Hold up "O") America was just coming out of the Great Depression. War was a threat and people had doubts about the future.

SECOND PERSON: (Hold up "D") In 1938, Mr. Berlin decided to "give something back" to the land he loved.

(Hold up "B") It was singer Kate Smith that asked Mr. Berlin to write a song that would "sort of wake up America."

THIRD PERSON: (Hold up "L") He first came up with two tunes but they just didn't quite do the job. Then he remembered a song he had sat aside 20 years before.

(Hold up "E") It was "God Bless America" originally written for the finale of a World War I army show, but never used.

FOURTH PERSON: (Hold up "S") Kate Smith introduced "God Bless America" on a program marking the 20th anniversary of the end of World War I.

(Hold up "S") The song quickly became the most popular song in the country.

FIFTH PERSON: (Hold up "A") It's composer, Irving Berlin, a longtime friend of Scouting, gave Boy Scouts of America royalties from the song.

(Hold up "M") In 1940 a trust fund was established for all royalties to go to Boy Scouts and Girl Scouts of America.

SIXTH PERSON: (Hold up "E") These funds have amounted to more than one million dollars over the years.

(Hold up "R") During World War II, it reflected the sense of national spirit that united America.

SEVENTH PERSON: (Hold up "I") It is still one of the best loved songs that show the spirit of America.

(Hold up "C") The song was introduced in November 1938.

EIGHTH PERSON: (Hold up "A") Will you please rise and join us as we sing, "God Bless America."

NATURE'S BEAUTY

SETTING: Eleven people will be needed to play the parts of nature. You will need three trees, two rocks, a frog, a covered bridge, a babbling brook, two bluebirds and an announcer. Trees; gently wave your arms as if the wind is blowing. Rocks; fold yourself up in a tight ball. Frog; squat down and "rib-bit." Covered bridge; cover yourself with a sheet or blanket. Babbling brook; sit on floor and make a sound like water flowing (bubbling noise). On cue the two bluebirds will run through the forest. Have some gentle music playing in the background to help set the mood. Begin to play before speaking and talk slowly with the music then continue to play for a minute after the announcer is done to convey the mood.

SCENE: The people will come out as they are introduced by the announcer and position themselves on the stage.

Announcer, give time for each part to position themselves before going on.

ANNOUNCER: Nature's beauty is all around us and sometimes we do not take the time to enjoy it. I would like to pause for a few minutes and help you paint a picture of a beautiful springtime day. Picture if you will–trees waving in the gentle breeze. On the ground are rocks of all sizes, shapes, and colors. Through the middle of our scene is a babbling brook. The peaceful flow of the water as it travels it path. At the waters edge is a frog quietly singing his song. Down the way is an old fashioned covered bridge waiting still for another boy to throw stones from it's edge. A quite, tranquil place to be when life's busy schedule keeps us running. Oh yes, here come the bluebirds. The bluebirds of happiness. What a pleasant way to end a day.

HOW THE TURKEY GOT HIS NAME

SETTING: Six people are needed for speaking parts and as many other people as you want. Have three dress as pilgrims and be husband, Keith East; wife, Penolope; and daughter, Prudence. Have two dress as Indians. One is offstage who makes the sounds of the strange bird. Any other number of Indians can be used. You will need a musket-type gun, bow and arrows, and a tomahawk.
SCENE: Pilgrims walk out onto the stage. Father East is carrying an imitation musket-type gun.

KEITH EAST: (To wife.) I believe I heard a noise, we may yet find a deer, dear, for our supper.
(Two Indians enter. Wife and Prudence scream and run behind Keith East.)

FIRST INDIAN: White man not be afraid. We friendly Indians.

KEITH EAST: How do we know you are friendly?

FIRST INDIAN: Ugh! Arrows have rubber tips (Toss a toy arrow out to show.)

PENELOPE: (Still frightened.) Yes, but what about him and that awful tomahawk?

SECOND INDIAN: Ugh! Cardboard!

FIRST INDIAN: White man have name?

KEITH EAST: My name is Keith East, but my friends call me Key.

SECOND INDIAN: O-key, Do-key. Go, Key! (He motions for the Pilgrims to cross in front of him.)

KEITH EAST: Before we leave, could you tell us where to... (He is interrupted by loud gobbling in woods behind him.)

STRANGE BIRD: (Makes loud gobbling noises.)

PRUDENCE: Daddy, Daddy, look! There's a great big funny bird in there. (Points to behind stage area.)

It's Showtime!

KEITH EAST: I wonder what it is?

FIRST INDIAN: Indians call him "Heap-good-eating-when-stuffed-gobble-gobble bird."

KEITH EAST: Ah, just the thing for dinner. (Raises musket and takes aim.)

PRUDENCE: No, no, Daddy! Don't shoot! Let me have it for a pet!

KEITH EAST: Nonsense, child! You know your mother would just have the work of taking care of it. (He aims again.)

PRUDENCE: No, no, Daddy! Maybe it will come if we call it. Daddy, every little child should have a pet. Call it to me!

PENELOPE: Yes, Key, I really think it would be nice for her.

KEITH EAST: Penelope, stop spoiling that child. If I call, it will be to get better aim. (Walks closer to where the noise came from.) Here, gobble-gobble.

STRANGE BIRD: (Gobbles back, but does not come out. Keith East prepares to shoot.)

PRUDENCE: (Screaming.) No, Daddy, call it to ME!

PENELOPE: Go on, Key. Call it to her. Please let's call it TUH HER, KEY!

PENELOPE AND INDIANS: (Repeating together.) Yes, let's call it TUH HER, KEY! Let's call it TUH HER, KEY!

KEITH EAST: And that is how the TUH HER KEY got it's name!

WHAT TIME IS IT?

SETTING: Two people are needed. Some sticks, stones, and string laying around the stage.
SCENE: The two people enter from opposite sides of the stage.

FIRST PERSON: Can you tell me what time it is?

SECOND PERSON: Sure! (Begins with sticks, and arranges them in front of him. Adds the string and stones as he works arranging them. Looks up to the sky as if to look at the sun, then says...) It's ____ (give correct time).

FIRST PERSON: Thanks, but, how did you do that? (Pointing to stones and sticks.)

SECOND PERSON: I just looked at my watch. (Holding up arm.)

HOW DO YOU GET TO SPUNKERVILLE?

SETTING: Six people are needed as follows: Two city folks, four farm folks – mom, dad, brother, sister. You will need a large cardboard car with handles for holding on to. The farm folks need to be dressed as farm people and act laid back, and kind of lazy. You will also need a bicycle horn.
SCENE: Mom is on stage sitting in an old chair taking it easy. The other farm folks are off stage. The two city folks drive up to the farm and honk their horn.

FIRST CITY PERSON: (Honks horn.) Excuse me, ma'am.
MOM: Hello there, what can I do for you?

FIRST CITY PERSON: We've been driving across these farm lands for hours and hours. Do you know how to get to Spunkerville?

MOM: Ya know, I'm not quite sure. Let me ask my son. Son?

BROTHER: (Comes out front.) Ya, ma?

MOM: Son, do you know the way to Spunkerville?

BROTHER: Not really. (Turns to yell for sis.) Hey, Sis! (She comes out.) Do you know the way to Spunkerville?

SISTER: Gee, I was there once, but that was a long time ago. I'll have to ask Pa. Hey, Pa! (Pa comes out.) Do you know how to get to Spunkerville?

PA: Let me see now. Once I had to go there for parts, but I'm not sure of how to get there from here.

It's Showtime!

RIDER CITY PERSON: Boy you people sure are dumb. You don't know anything do you?

PA: Well, I see it like this. We may not be very smart, but at least we're not lost!

STIFF NECK

SETTING: Five people are needed. No special props are needed.
SCENE: Each person follows the one ahead of him and talks on cue.

FIRST PERSON: (Enters looking up, walks over to other side of stage and stares at ceiling.)

SECOND PERSON: (Enters, looks at first person, then starts looking into air with him.)

THIRD PERSON, FOURTH PERSON, and FIFTH PERSON come in and do the same.

FIFTH PERSON: (To the fourth person.) Excuse me, but what are we looking at?

FOURTH PERSON: I don't know, I'll ask. (To the third person.) What are we looking at?

THIRD PERSON: I don't know, I'll ask. (To the second person.) What are we looking at?

SECOND PERSON: I don't know, I'll ask. (To the first person.) What are we looking at?

FIRST PERSON: I don't know. As for me, I have a stiff neck.

BAWL GAME

SETTING: Five people are needed dressed in clown make-up and colorful shirts.
SCENE: A clown comes on stage crying. Soon, three others come on crying.

The last clown is not crying and he is the first person to speak.

FIRST PERSON: What's the matter with you guys?

SECOND PERSON: We've been to a bawl game.

FIRST PERSON: Ball Game? I don't understand, did your team lose?

THIRD PERSON: It wasn't that kind of ball game. It was a crying game!

FIRST PERSON: Crying game?

FOURTH PERSON: Yes, to see who could cry the best.

FIRST PERSON: Well, did you?

FIFTH PERSON: No. . . we lost, that's why we're bawling!

THE CHRISTMAS PRESENT

SETTING: Nine people are needed with one dressed as Santa Claus and one dressed as a big shabby box.
SCENE: Santa Claus and the box come onto stage. Other people will come on one at a time.

SANTA: I'll leave you here on this street and maybe someone will take you home this year.

BOX: I hope so, I'll get busy right away trying to make someone take me home.

(First person enters.)
BOX: Please, will you take me home as a Christmas present?

FIRST PERSON: My mother would really yell if I brought a funny thing like you home! (Person leaves.)

(Second person enters.)
BOX: Please, will you take me home as a Christmas present?

It's Showtime!

SECOND PERSON: Are you serious? I wouldn't take anything as dirty as you for a present. (Person leaves.)

(Third person enters.)
BOX: Please, will you take me home as a Christmas present?

THIRD PERSON: Nah, I want a new baseball glove. (Person leaves.)

(Fourth person enters.)
BOX: Please, will you take me home as a Christmas present?

FOURTH PERSON: Of course not! I don't pick up strange things off the street! (Person leaves.)

(Fifth person enters.)
BOX: Please, will you take me home as a Christmas present?

FIFTH PERSON: I should put you in a trash can. You're littering the street. (Person leaves.)

(Sixth person enters.)
BOX: Please, will you take me home as a Christmas present?

SIXTH PERSON: Kids want presents that are new. (Person leaves.)

(Seventh person enters.)
BOX: Please, will you take me home as a Christmas present?

SEVENTH PERSON: I don't want you and it looks like nobody else does either! (Person leaves.)

(Santa enters.)
SANTA: Well, I see you didn't get anyone to take you again this year.

BOX: I haven't given up hope. Someday someone will take me home.

SANTA: You know, I've been hauling you back and forth so long I've forgotten what you are.

BOX: I'm not sure, but when God packed me up nearly 2,000 years ago, he called me "Peace On Earth."

ORDER IN THE COURTROOM!

SETTING: Five people are needed with two being selected as a judge and prosecutor. Other people are the defendants. You need a chair for the judge, and a clipboard with papers on it for the prosecutor.
SCENE: In the court room with the defendants sitting down.

JUDGE: Order in the court. On this day "Pets Against Owners" have several complaints that need to be addressed. The court is ready to hear from the prosecutor.

(One person comes forward with the prosecutor.)

PROSECUTOR: This owner is charged with failure to sufficiently exercise his dog. The dog has been seen just laying around the backyard all the time.

JUDGE: This court finds the defendant guilty. Your sentence is, 'Your bed will be full of dog hairs for 60 days.' Next case.

(Another person comes forward.)

PROSECUTOR: This owner is charged with failure to feed his cat nutritional cat food. Instead, the cat has been seen roaming the neighborhood for food.

It's Showtime!

JUDGE: This court finds the defendant guilty. Your sentence is, 'To feed your cat in bed for 90 days.' Next case.

(Last person comes forward. In this case, the last person needs to interrupt several times, protesting. Saying things like, "but I never," "let me explain," "if you will just listen." The prosecution just continues with the charges.)

PROSECUTOR: This is the worst case the courts have ever seen. The owner makes his dog sit in one position all day. The dog never gets fed. The owner plays ball using the dog as the ball. Worst of all, instead of bathing his dog, the owner throws him in the washing machine and sets the machine on "fluff dry."

(The people there gasp in horror. They then begin to mumble among themselves.)

JUDGE: Silence in this court room! Those surely are the worst I have ever heard! Do you have anything to say?

LAST PERSON: Yes! What I've been trying to tell you is, my dog is a "Stuffed Toy!"

SHAKE WELL

SETTING: Two people are needed.
SCENE: One is on stage shaking his whole body. In walks the other person.

FIRST PERSON: What's the matter with you?

SECOND PERSON: I've got to take my medicine as soon as this program is over.

FIRST PERSON: Well, what's the matter?

SECOND PERSON: You see that bottle over there? (Points off stage.)

FIRST PERSON: Yes.

SECOND PERSON: It says, "SHAKE WELL BEFORE TAKING."

THOSE IMPORTANT PAPERS

SETTING: Six people are needed. One is the villain who is dressed in black, with a black hat and mustache. Another is dressed as a girl as the heroine. You will need some play money, a deed to the town, and a claim to the Gold Mine. Others can be wearing cowboy clothes and hats.

SCENE: Place a cardboard set of railroad tracks in front of the people and have a railroad crossing sign standing up beside them. The villain and the girl should be on stage in front of the tracks. Others enter one at a time.

FIRST PERSON: (Villain) Give me the important papers I seek or I'll tie you to the track!

SECOND PERSON: (Heroine) What do you mean? I have nothing to give you! Help! Someone, help!

THIRD PERSON: I'll save you. Here is the money to pay off the house mortgage.

FIRST PERSON: These are not the important papers. (Throws them to the side.) Now go and get what I ask or I'll tie her to the tracks!

SECOND PERSON: (Screams in fright.) Help! Help! Someone please, help me!

FOURTH PERSON: I'll save you. Here, Mr. Villain, is the deed to the town.

FIRST PERSON: (Raises voice a little louder.) What? I don't need any town papers! I own this town already. I want the important paper! (Pretends to tie heroin to tracks.)

SECOND PERSON: (Raises voice a little louder.) Won't someone please help me?

FIFTH PERSON: (Comes running in.) Here, here! Take the claim to the Gold Mine!

FIRST PERSON: I don't want no Gold Mine papers! These are still not the important papers!

SECOND PERSON: I hear a train! Oh, No! HELP! HELP!

SIXTH PERSON: (Comes running in.) Wait! I have the papers you seek! (Hands villain a roll of toilet paper.)

FIRST PERSON: Now these are the important papers I have been waiting for! (Grabs paper and runs off stage.)

SECOND PERSON: (Hugs hero.) My hero! (Others gather around and all walk off stage.)

RUN-ONS and KNOCK-KNOCK JOKES

Run-Ons or Knock-Knock jokes can make people feel happy. They are silly jokes or one-liners that make you stop and think for just a moment, then smile. Here are a few that can be used in and out of a program to help break the ice and add some flare.

A prop that we used for several programs was a club house. We made it from a large refrigerator box. It had working windows and doors. It was spray painted and we used markers to make it look like a wooden house. Over the door were the words "Club house." We cut about six windows, two on the front and two on each side that were different sizes. We tied rope to each window and door to make it open and close. There was a large door in the back where the people came in and went out. As we prepared for the run-ons, people would get inside and get into position. They then would take turns opening the windows or front door to do their lines. Sometimes people would come up to the front door and really knock for the jokes. This proved to be a big hit with everyone. Give it a try.

FIRST PERSON: Hey (name of person), what did one eye say to the other eye?
SECOND PERSON: I dunno, what?
FIRST PERSON: Just between you and me, something smells!

FIRST PERSON: Knock-Knock.
SECOND PERSON: Who's there?
FIRST PERSON: Doris.
SECOND PERSON: Doris, who?
FIRST PERSON: Doris locked, so I had to knock!

FIRST PERSON: Is it true that an alligator won't attack you if you carry a flashlight?
SECOND PERSON: It depends on how fast you carry it!

FIRST PERSON: Mr. Pet Store owner, I want to buy a dog. How much are these puppies?
SECOND PERSON: They are $5.00 a piece.
FIRST PERSON: Oh, but I wanted a whole one!

FIRST PERSON: What do you call a rabbit with fleas?
SECOND PERSON: I don't know.
FIRST PERSON: Bugs Bunny.

FIRST PERSON: What begins with an "E" and ends with an "E" and has a letter between it?
SECOND PERSON: I have no idea, tell me!
FIRST PERSON: An envelope.

FIRST PERSON: Hey, look at your campfire!
SECOND PERSON: What about it?
FIRST PERSON: It is still smoking.
SECOND PERSON: Well, it can't chew!

FIRST PERSON: Knock-Knock.
SECOND PERSON: Who's there?
FIRST PERSON: Sarasota.
SECOND PERSON: Sarasota, who?
FIRST PERSON: Sarasota machine around here?

FIRST PERSON: When will the rain stop falling?
SECOND PERSON: I don't know.
FIRST PERSON: When it hits the ground.

FIRST PERSON: When is a black dog most likely to enter a house?
SECOND PERSON: You got me, when?
FIRST PERSON: When the door is open.

FIRST PERSON: Hey, can you use the word "detour" in a sentence?
SECOND PERSON: Sure... De guide took us on "detour" of de museum!

FIRST PERSON: I heard you left your last job. Why?
SECOND PERSON: Illness.
FIRST PERSON: What was wrong?
SECOND PERSON: The camp director got sick of me!

FIRST PERSON: I have been seeing spots before my eyes!
SECOND PERSON: Have you seen a doctor?
FIRST PERSON: No, just those spots.

FIRST PERSON: Doctor, Doctor, I keep thinking I'm a horse!
SECOND PERSON: It's O.K. son, I can cure you. But it will take a lot of money.
FIRST PERSON: Money's no problem. I just won the Kentucky Derby!

FIRST PERSON: I wonder what it would be like to be a piece of wood?
SECOND PERSON: It probably would be "board."

FIRST PERSON: I hear you have been taking a lot of training to help you in your job.
SECOND PERSON: Yes, I have been going three nights a week.
FIRST PERSON: Well, how was that memory course you took?
SECOND PERSON: What memory course?

Run-Ons And Knock-Knock Jokes

FIRST PERSON: Hey, what is the best way to avoid infection caused by biting ticks and spiders?
SECOND PERSON: Don't bite any!

FIRST PERSON: Are you sure this waterfront is safe for the kids to go swimming?
SECOND PERSON: I sure am!
FIRST PERSON: You sure there are no water moccasins around?
SECOND PERSON: Positive! The alligators scared them all away!

FIRST PERSON: How come you didn't stay for the second part of the play?
SECOND PERSON: I couldn't wait! The program said it took place a year later.

FIRST PERSON: Hey, are you going to Sam's birthday party?
SECOND PERSON: Well, I was. But the invitation said four to seven - and I'm nine!

FIRST PERSON: Can you tell me what happens when a cement truck hits a police van carrying prisoners?
SECOND PERSON: No, I can't. What happens?
FIRST PERSON: In no time, you have "hardened" criminals!

FIRST PERSON: Knock, knock.
SECOND PERSON: Who's there?
FIRST PERSON: Wheel.
SECOND PERSON: Wheel who?
FIRST PERSON: Open the door and wheel stop.

FIRST PERSON: What is it called when a ghost robs a bank?
SECOND PERSON: I dunno, What is it called?
FIRST PERSON: A poltergeist!

FIRST PERSON: Hey, guess what? I got a hundred in school today!
SECOND PERSON: That's great! In what subject?
FIRST PERSON: In two subjects! A 40 in Spelling and a 60 in Math!

FIRST PERSON: Did you know about the job opening as a garbage collector? Do you have any experience?
SECOND PERSON: No, but I'll pick it up as I go along.

FIRST PERSON: Doctor, doctor!
SECOND PERSON: Yes, may I help you?
FIRST PERSON: I broke my arm in four places!
SECOND PERSON: Well, then, stay out of those places!

FIRST PERSON: Can you use the word "believing" in a sentence?
SECOND PERSON: Sure...The lunch bell just rang, so if you don't mind, I'll "believing."

FIRST PERSON: Knock, knock.
SECOND PERSON: Who's there?
FIRST PERSON: Diploma.
SECOND PERSON: Diploma, who?
FIRST PERSON: Diploma is coming to fix the sink.

FIRST PERSON: (On stage as second person comes in pulling a rope.) Hey, why are you pulling that rope across the stage?
SECOND PERSON: (Says as he comes on stage.) Well, have you ever tried pushing a rope!

FIRST PERSON: What do you call a nervous cow?
SECOND PERSON: I don't know, what?
FIRST PERSON: Beef jerky!

FIRST PERSON: Gosh, I lost my cat.
SECOND PERSON: How about putting an ad in the newspaper under "Lost & Found?"
FIRST PERSON: No, that wouldn't do any good. My cat can't read.

FIRST PERSON: Knock, knock.
SECOND PERSON: Who's there?
FIRST PERSON: Budget.
SECOND PERSON: Budget, who?
FIRST PERSON: If you will budget, I bet I can get through the door.

FIRST PERSON: Excuse me, doctor. My friend was hit by a steamroller. Can you tell what room he is in?
SECOND PERSON: Absolutely. Rooms 202, 203, 204, and 205.

FIRST PERSON: You know, I've always heard that the best way to learn anything is to start at the bottom.
SECOND PERSON: Yeah, except when you want to learn to swim!

FIRST PERSON: Knock, knock.
SECOND PERSON: Who's there?
FIRST PERSON: Otter.
SECOND PERSON: Otter, who?
FIRST PERSON: After all these knock-knock jokes, we otter at least apologize.

FIRST PERSON: How many fish did you catch Saturday?
SECOND PERSON: I caught six beauties! Why?
FIRST PERSON: Just as I thought! The fish market is tying to bill us for eight!

FIRST PERSON: Knock, knock.
SECOND PERSON: Who's there?
FIRST PERSON: Data.
SECOND PERSON: Data, who?
FIRST PERSON: Data tough hike we had to do today.

FIRST PERSON: Can you explain the meaning of the word "retire?"
SECOND PERSON: Sure...that's what someone does when a bicycle tire goes flat!

FIRST PERSON: Do you know how to keep a fish from smelling?
SECOND PERSON: No, I do not. How?
FIRST PERSON: Cut off his nose.

FIRST PERSON: Well, it looks like history has repeated itself.
SECOND PERSON: What do you mean?
FIRST PERSON: I mean, I got another "D" in it!

FIRST PERSON: Did you know that it takes six sheep to make one wool sweater?
SECOND PERSON: That's odd, I didn't even know sheep could knit!

FIRST PERSON: Mom is gonna help me bake my new invention–a metric cookie.
SECOND PERSON: Great. What will you call it?
FIRST PERSON: I'm gonna call it a "gram cracker."

FIRST PERSON: My silly brother did it again!
SECOND PERSON: What happened?
FIRST PERSON: He wanted to see the polar bears, so he went to the zoo. But when he got to the zoo's entrance, the sidewalk forked. A sign read: Bear Left, so he came home disappointed.

FIRST PERSON: Why did the mother rope get mad at the baby rope?
SECOND PERSON: I don't know. Why did she get mad?
FIRST PERSON: Because he had been knotty!

FIRST PERSON: I bet you didn't know that Davy Crockett had three ears.
SECOND PERSON: Three, are you sure?
FIRST PERSON: Yea. He had a right ear. He had a left ear. And he had a "wild frontier!"

FIRST PERSON: What did the mother ghost say to the baby ghost when they got in the car?
SECOND PERSON: I don't know, what?
FIRST PERSON: Fasten your sheet belt.

FIRST PERSON: Why did all the elephants go on strike at the zoo?
SECOND PERSON: I do not know, why?
FIRST PERSON: They were tired of working for peanuts.

FIRST PERSON: Do you know why Larry really became a shoemaker?
SECOND PERSON: I haven't heard. Why?
FIRST PERSON: Because he really likes "sole" music.

FIRST PERSON: Why does that baseball player always wear a mask?
SECOND PERSON: Because he is always "stealing bases!"

FIRST PERSON: I was up all night last night running around in the forest.
SECOND PERSON: For ever more, why?
FIRST PERSON: I couldn't remember something and was trying to jog my memory.

FIRST PERSON: Knock, knock.
SECOND PERSON: Who's there?
FIRST PERSON: Diesel.
SECOND PERSON: Diesel, who?
FIRST PERSON: Disel be the last knock–knock joke for the day.

INDEX

INTRODUCTION
Opening, Props, Scenery iii
Make-Up, Costumes, Areas Of Concern iv
Let's Write A Skit v

IT'S SHOW TIME!
A Fool's Gold 36
All Aboard! 22
The Atlantic Trip 4

Baked Alaska 23
Balloon Madness 20
Baseball Throwing Contest 2
Bawl Game 53
Beach Bummer 27
Bird Watchers 15
Bird Watching Pun 10
Bon Voyage 8
Broken Lawnmower 30
Buc Tuocs 12

Christmas Around The World 46
Christmas Carols 32
The Christmas Present 54
Confused Drummer 38

Defective Nails 9

Extra, Extra! 26

The Flea Circus 17
The Forgotten Treasure 45

Freedom 19

General Custer 27
God Bless America 47

Helping Hands 16
Higher Court 31
Hillbilly Family 21
How Do You Get To Spunkerville? 52
How The Turkey Got His Name 50

I Am An American 40
The Infantry 5

Jelly Beans 34

Kayak Trouble 2

Lion Tamer 8
The Liberty Bell 24

Many Muscles 39

Nature's Beauty 49

On The Line 26
Order In The Court Room 56
The Other Side Of The Mountain 14

Peace Be With You 21
Pumpkin Pie Patch 28

Railroad Crossing 3
The Redcoats Are Coming! 16

Shake Well 57
The Six Ships Of Scouting 13

INDEX

Some Beach 41
The Special Picnic 18
Stiff Neck 53

There Is A Bear 6
This Is Your Life! 43
Those Important Papers 58
Torn Paper 7

Vindow Viper 33

Weary Traveler 11
Welcome To Our Neighborhood 42
What Time Is It? 51
Wrong Feet 33

RUN-ONS AND KNOCK-KNOCK JOKES
A collection of over 40 run-ons and jokes 60